Sexicon

The Ultimate X-Rated Dictionary

Rod L. Evans, Ph.D.

CITADEL PRESS
Kensington Publishing Corp.
www.kensingtonbooks.com

CITADEL PRESS BOOKS are published by

Kensington Publishing Corp.
850 Third Avenue
New York, NY 10022

Copyright © 2002 Rod L. Evans, Ph.D.

All Kensington titles, imprints, and distributed lines are available at special quantity discounts for bulk purchases for sales promotions, premiums, fund-raising, educational, or institutional use. Special book excerpts or customized printings can also be created to fit specific needs. For details, write or phone the office of the Kensington special sales manager: Kensington Publishing Corp., 850 Third Avenue, New York, NY 10022, attn: Special Sales Department, phone 1-800-221-2647.

First Printing: February 2002

10 9 8 7 6 5 4 3 2 1

Printed in the United States of America

Library of Congress Control Number: 2001098950

ISBN 0-8065-2307-7

Sexicon

The Ultimate X-Rated Dictionary

CONTENTS

ACKNOWLEDGMENTS

Many thanks to those who helped me: to Robin Hudgins, who tirelessly and professionally typed the manuscript; to Abbott Saks, who encouraged me and suggested the help of Hope Mihalap; to Dr. Roy Aycock, who introduced me to both Dr. Phil Hines, who helped with many pronunciations, and Hope Mihalap, who helped with all the pronunciations; to my editor, Richard Ember, who enthusiastically supported me, and to the other staff at Kensington who helped produce this book; to my literary agent's assistant, Janet Rosen, who helped place the book with a publisher, and, finally, to my literary agent, Sheree Bykofsky, who has always believed in me and displayed a cheerful professionalism.

Although I gratefully acknowledge the help that I have received in creating this work, I take full responsibility for its contents.

Rod L. Evans

INTRODUCTION

Few subjects are as compelling and arresting as sex, and no language has a larger vocabulary for describing the world, including the world of sex, than English. Yet most English-users continue to overuse hackneyed four-letter words that often no longer shock people. Many sexual words belong to slang and were colorful when first used, but have become dated and sometimes obscure. Other sexual words belong to current slang but are obscene and hackneyed. While sexual slang is often versatile, describing a wide range of sexual practices and tastes, it sometimes lacks terms for highly unusual tastes and preferences. For example, so far as this author knows, there is no English slang term for the specific attraction many men have for women in high heels. Fortunately, because English has freely borrowed from numerous languages, including Greek and Latin, there is a word for that specific attraction. Unfortunately, though, you would be hard pressed to find it—at least outside a highly specialized dictionary. The word, by the way, is **altocalciphilia,** derived from Latin words *altus* (high) and *calcis* (heel), and the Greek word *philia* (attachment, attraction, fondness).

A goal of this dictionary is to help remedy the problem by presenting definitions of hundreds of obscure but delightfully descriptive words for sexual tastes and behavior, including tastes and behavior that would qualify as kinky even in the wildest Roman orgy. Even though most of even the kinkiest human sexual behavior has analogues in the animal kingdom, we human beings, unlike other animals, have created countless rules, often varying among cultures, for what counts as "natural" and "unnatural" desires and behavior. Words describing "unnatural acts and preferences" are often funny because of the often-ambivalent attitudes people have toward sex. We are simultaneously attracted to, and repelled by, "forbidden sex," and some creative capitalists, not least Madonna, have become rich by taking advantage of that ambivalence.

This book defines potentially useful words whose meanings are entertaining by themselves but are little known. The meaning of each term is given, with brief comments about its derivation, followed by an illustrative and often humorous sentence. Because the terms are obscure, and because they are often derived from Greek or Latin, they usually do not sound sexual or "dirty." Consequently, someone who uses them can talk dirty without getting caught, as when a man can compliment a woman for having an attractive rump by calling her **callipygian**, from Greek words for "beautiful," *kalos*, and "buttocks," *pyge*.

If you do, however, want to get caught, you can use the words instructively, as when you might say: "Howard was masturbating while watching the dogs mate, revealing his **mixoscopic zoophilia**." The expression "mixoscopic zoophilia" designates, predictably from the context just given, sexual arousal from watching sexual activities of animals, as when people "get off by watching animals get it on." That expression, by the way, was used by psychologist and pioneering sexual researcher Havelock Ellis, in his classic seven-volume *Studies in the Psychology of Sex,* originally published between 1897 and 1928. Some of the terms in this dictionary are more recent coinages than "mixoscopic zoophilia," and some are much older, but they are all delightfully descriptive.

HOW TO USE THIS BOOK

You can use this dictionary in two main ways. First, you can simply pick it up and begin reading anywhere. On any page you'll find fascinating words that you probably never knew existed. Second, you can find a word by looking at its definition in the reverse dictionary (reversicon) at the end of the book.

USING THE REVERSICON

Although dictionaries usually list the words to be defined in alphabetical order, a reversicon lists definitions or descriptions of concepts in alphabetical order, and then provides words fitting those definitions. That reverse format is especially helpful when looking for words that are much more obscure than their definitions. For example, suppose you want to find a word meaning "possessing beautiful breasts." Though that idea or meaning is well known, most people will probably not know a particular English word (especially one outside slang) carrying that meaning. Incidentally, even many slang expressions (including "stacked") will not quite suffice. If you look in the reversicon under "Breast," you'll see the definition "possessing beautiful breasts," beside which you'll see **callimastian**. Should you want to learn more about "callimastian," including its roots and pronunciation, as well as a sentence illustrating its use, you can simply look it up in the main part of this book. The reversicon is also helpful for fixing the word in your mind, since it is usually easier to learn families of related words than lists of unrelated words.

When you see a heading in the reversicon, for example, for example, "Beautiful," that heading will include a horizontal line ___,

HOW TO USE THIS BOOK

making "(Beautiful ___)." Whenever you see that line before or after words of a definition, read the line as if it is the heading-word or heading-phrase. For example, a definition under the "Beautiful" heading might be presented as "possessing ___ buttocks." You would read that phrase as "possessing beautiful buttocks," and you would find that the word "callipygian" fits the definition.

Most of the words in this dictionary are nouns or adjectives. The context provided, including sentences illustrating the words, will usually make the part of speech quite easy to identify.

A NOTE ON PRONUNCIATION
AND WORD ORIGINS

I have provided the pronunciations of most words in this dictionary. Since most of the words are rarely spoken, and because a number of them are neologisms (new coinages), the pronunciations are often only approximate. It is well to remember that the study of pronunciation is at least as much an art as a science, since well-educated speakers even from the same geographical region sometimes pronounce the same words differently, and persons from different regions often pronounce even some everyday words differently. Further, some unusual words, such as "contumely" (rudeness or contempt stemming from arrogance), can have three or more acceptable pronunciations.

When giving the pronunciations for rare and obscure words, including even "orthoepy" (the study of pronunciations), authorities can differ. Some orthoepists pronounce their speciality with an emphasis on the "or," while others stress the "tho." Ironically, persons who specialize in the study of pronunciations cannot agree on a standard pronunciation for the name of their field, much as philosophers cannot agree on what philosophy is supposed to study.

In creating this book, I consulted several different authorities, including such excellent dictionaries as *Webster's Third New International Dictionary* and *The American Heritage Dictionary of the English Language*, as well as students of language. Where possible, I have tried to be guided by reliable authorities, but realize that giving pronunciations for rare and obscure words, including neologisms, is tricky. I believe that, although some of the pronunciations given will be rejected by some scholars, most of the pronunciations are serviceable and, I think or hope, defensible. I have also provided brief indications of the origins of the roots.

CAPitalized LETters INdicate the ACcented PORtion of the word, with secondary accents some*times* indicated by italics

VOWELS

CONSONANTS

a	**a**ct		b	**b**aby
ā	l**a**te		ch	**ch**urch
ä	f**a**ther		d	**d**oor
e	m**e**n		f	**f**ar
er	**air**		g	**g**as
ē	tr**ee**		h	be**h**ind
ēr	**near**		j	**j**ar
i	d**i**g		k	**k**elp
ī	k**i**te		l	nai**l**
o	p**o**t		m	ra**m**
ō	m**oa**n		n	**n**ice
ô	p**aw**		ng	ha**ng**
oi	t**oi**l		p	ste**p**
o͝o	b**oo**k		r	**r**at
o͞o	**oo**h		s	**s**ee
ou	**out**		sh	wi**sh**
u	p**u**p		t	**t**eam
ū	**u**nique		*th*	***th***in
ur	ne**r**d		th	lea**th**er
ə	**a**bove		v	**v**oice
			w	**w**ine
			y	**y**es
			z	**z**ebra
			zh	a**zu**re

Sexicon

A

acanthophallic (ə-*kan*-thə-FAL-ik): having a rough or spiny penis. Derived from Greek *akantha* (thorn) and *phallos* (penis).

*Michelle complained that her boyfriend is so **acanthophallic** that having sex with him is like having sex with a porcupine.*

acedolagnia (a-*sē*-dō-LAG-nē-ə): complete indifference to sexual matters, widely considered more common among women than men. Derived from Greek *a-* (without), *kedos* (care), and *lagneia* (lust).

When the Jeff Goldblum character in The Big Chill *said "Everybody does everything in order to get laid," he was overlooking a distinct minority of persons with **acedolagnia**.*

achlysio (*a*-KLĒ-sē-ō): mild state of mental drowsiness following a long and satisfying sexual bout. Derived from Achlys (goddess of obscurity), related to the Greek *achlys* (mist, darkness).

*After a stressful day, the man enjoyed the release provided by the **achlysio** following his vigorous lovemaking with his wife.*

acmegenesis (*ak*-mi/mə-JEN-i-sis): the induction of orgasm. Derived from Greek *akme* (highest point) and *gignesthai* (to be born).

*Ridgely said that he can enjoy sex without experiencing orgasm, especially when he induces **acmegenesis** in his wife.*

acokoinonia (ə-kō-koi-NŌ-nē-ə): sexual intercourse without sexual desire, as when people engage in sex out of habit or duty rather than out of desire. Derived from Greek *a-* (without), Latin *conatus* (desire, impulse), and Greek *koinonia* (sexual intercourse).

*Because Carol's libido had weakened over the years, and because she was no longer attracted to her husband, her sexual relations were reduced to **acokoinonia**.*

acomoclitic (ə-komə-KLIT-ik): preferring a hairless vulva, as from aesthetic reasons, or because of a phobia. Derived from Greek *a-* (without), *kome* (hair), and *klinein* (to lean).

There are pornographic movies and magazines with such titles as Shaved Babes, *designed to appeal to* **acomoclitic** *men.*

acomovulvate (ə-komə-VUL-vāt): of women, having no pubic hair. Derived from Greek *a-* (without), Greek *kome* (hair), and Latin *vulva* (external female genitalia).
Although some men enjoy sexual relations with **acomovulvate** *women, others consider their condition "unnatural."*

aconorrhea (ə-kon-ō-RĒ-ə): a discharge of seminal fluid due not to a conscious sexual orgasm but to other causes, as when a man is mildly excited by some stimulus, such as a woman's legs; the discharge is often unnoticed at the time. Derived from Greek *a-* (without), Latin *conatus* (desire, impulse), and Greek *rheo* (anything flowing, such as a stream).
The adolescent male was distressed to see evidence of his **aconorrhea** *on his underwear.*

acousticophilia (ə-ko͞o-sti-kō/kə-FIL-ē-ə): arousal from sounds, not only music (*see* **melolagnia**) but also sexual commands, love poems, screaming, panting, sighing, groaning, and so on. Derived from Greek *akoustikos* (pertaining to hearing) and *philia* (attachment, attraction).
Michelle's **acousticophilia** *led her to play her favorite CDs whenever she was with her boyfriend.*

acrasolagnia (ə-*kra*-zō-LAG-nē-ə): lack of sexual self-control. Derived from Greek *a-* (without), *kratos* (power), and *lagneia* (lust).
The gossip columnist submitted that Madonna has always been highly selective in her romantic contacts, and that her persona of **acrasolagnia** *was simply ingenious marketing.*

acritition (a-kri-TISH-ən): sexual intercourse ending without orgasm. Derived from Greek *a-* (without), Greek *krisis* (crisis), and Latin *coition* (intercourse).
Because the young man was taught that 'real men' always climax during sex, he felt embarrassed by his **acritition**.

acrocoition (akrō-kō-ISHəN): the habit of indulging in sexual intercourse with excessive frequency. Derived from Greek *akros* (highest) and Latin *coitus* (sexual intercourse).
Many people wonder whether the **acrocoition** *of rock stars and politicians is due more to the easy availability of potential sexual partners than to the narcissism and hypersexuality of those who gravitate toward those occupations.*

acrophilia (ak-rə-FIL-ē-ə): the tendency to be sexually aroused by heights. Derived from Greek *akros* (highest) and *philia* (attachment, attraction). Acrophilia can prompt people to have sex at high altitudes, as on an airplane, where those who have sex can qualify for membership in the facetious "mile-high club." Other people with the tendency under discussion will sometimes climb ladders blindfolded in S&M (sadomasochistic) games, or will seek out sky diving and bungy jumping, though not everyone who sky dives or bungy jumps would describe the feelings and sensations attendant upon those activities as sexual.

Jason's **acrophilia** *led him to have sex while he was suspended from the top of a lighthouse.*

acrorthosis (*ak*-ror-THŌ-səs): the condition of having erections with abnormal frequency. Derived from Greek *akros* (highest) and *orthosis* (a straightening).

When someone asked the young actor why he felt the need to have dozens of sexual encounters with different women, he said that he wanted to make constructive use of his **acrorthosis***.*

acrotomophilia (ak-rə-tō-mō-FIL-ē-ə): arousal from thinking of one's sexual partner as an amputee. Derived from Greek *akros* (highest), *tomos* (a cutting), and *philia* (attachment, attraction).

When Ida learned about Melvin's **acrotomophilia***, she called him "a sick puppy," and accused him of being incapable of fully appreciating a woman with all her appendages.*

acucullophallia (ə-kū-kul-lō-FAL-ē-ə): the condition of having a circumcised penis. Derived from Greek *a-* (without), Latin *cucullus* (hood), and Greek *phallos* (penis).

Although **acucullophallia** *has been important to Jews for thousands of years, and slightly lowers the risk of certain diseases, some people regard it as a product of mutilation.*

acucullophallic (ə-kū-kul-lō-FAL-ik): having, or relating to, a circumcised penis. Derived from Greek *a-* (without), Latin *cucullus* (hood), and Greek *phallos* (penis).

Becky preferred **acucullophallic** *men because she found their penises less "cheesy" than those of uncircumcised men.*

acucullophilia (ə-kū-kul-lō-FIL-ē-ə): fondness for circumcised penises. Derived from Greek *a-* (without), Latin *cucullus* (hood), and Greek *philia* (attachment, attraction).

*Because of Melissa's **acucullophilia**, she preferred to travel in the United States and Israel.*

acucullus (ə-kū-KUL-is): an uncircumcised penis. Derived from Greek *a-* (without) and Latin *cucullus* (hood).

*The drunken Jewish nymphomaniac shouted, "I need an **acucullus**, pronto!" and then passed out.*

aculeophallic (ə-kū-lē-ō-FAL-ik): having a pointed or conical penis. Derived from Latin *aculeus* (point) and Greek *phallos* (penis).

*Tipper's husband, Al, was so **aculeophallic** that she felt gored whenever they would have sex.*

adamite: an obsolete term for a nudist. Derived from the name of a Christian sect in Germany and Holland (the Adamites) whose members practiced virtual nudity and extramarital sexual intercourse at their secret meetings, believing that, as God's chosen, they had been reborn into a state of innocence in which all the elected were commanded to love one another.

*Current **adamites**, unlike the original ones in Germany and Holland, are more likely to play volleyball than to have sex.*

adectia (ə-DEK-tē-ə): the unwillingness or inability of a woman to accept the male in intercourse. Derived from Latin *a-* (not) and Greek *dektos* (acceptable).

*Because Raymond was almost always interested in sex, he decided against dating Laura again when he found out about her **adectia**.*

adelophilia (ə-del-ō-FIL-ē-ə): giving the false impression that one is not interested in sexual matters, a word applied especially to women. Derived from Greek *adelos* (not evident) and *philia* (attachment, attraction).

*We were stunned to learn that our mousy librarian was an insatiable "swinger" whose **adelophilia** was adopted to distract people from her private life.*

adelphepothia (ə-del-fe/fə-PÄ-thē-ə): sexual interest in one's sister. Derived from Greek *adelphe* (sister) and *pothos* (fond desire).

*We could not imagine anyone affected by **adelphepothia**, even if his sister looked like Julia Roberts.*

adelphirexia (ə-del-fi-REKS-ē-ə): sexual desire for one's nephew. Derived from Greek *adelphideos* (nephew) and Latin/Greek *orexis* (desire, appetite).

*The teenaged girl said that she could succumb to **adelphirexia** if her nephew were Tom Cruise.*

adventitious erogenesis (*ad*-ven-TISH-əs irō-JEN-i-sis): sexual excitement, often accompanied by ejaculation, due to emotions usually not associated with libido, such as fear or anger. Derived from Latin *adventicius* (coming in addition, designating the idea of having an outside source), Greek *eros* (sexual love), and Greek *gignesthai* (to be born).

*We could make at least some sense of **adventitious erogenesis** because we could understand how extreme emotion, such as terror, might stimulate people sexually.*

agenobiosis (ə-*jen*-ō-bī-Ō-sis): the condition in which a married couple agree to live together without sex. Derived from Greek *a-* (without), *gen-* (birth, cause, kind), *bio-* (life), *-osis* (condition).

*For various reasons, two persons who are not interested in each other sexually will sometimes marry and engage in **agenobiosis**.*

agonophilia (ə-gon-ə-FIL-ē-ə): arousal from a sexual partner's pretended struggle. Derived from Greek *a-* (without), *agon* (struggle, gathering assembly), and *philia* (attachment, attraction).

*Because of Marla's assertiveness and John's desire to be dominated, Marla enjoyed indulging her **agonophilia** in their sexual relations.*

agoraphilia (*ägorə*-FIL-ē-ə): arousal from being in open spaces, or having sex in public. Derived from Greek *agora* (marketplace, place of assembly) and *philia* (attachment, attraction).

*We did not learn of the couple's **agoraphilia** until we saw them having sex in the parking lot.*

agrexophilia (ə-*greks*-ə-FIL-ē-ə): arousal from knowing that others are observing or hearing one's having sex. Derived from Latin *ad* (toward), *grex* (flock), and Greek *philia* (attachment, attraction).

*Their **agrexophilia** led the couple to shake the bed while they were having sex so that their neighbors in the apartments could hear them.*

agrexophrenia (ə-*greks*-ə-FRĒN-ē-ə): the inability to perform sexual intercourse because of knowing that someone is nearby, as in an adjoining room. Derived from Latin *ad* (toward), *grex* (flock), and Greek *phren* (mind).

*Because of his **agrexophrenia**, Darrin could not make love to Samantha while Samantha's mother was in the adjoining bedroom.*

agynophelimity (ə-*ji/gī*-nō-fe/fə-LIM-i-tē): the female inability to give sexual satisfaction. Derived from Greek *a-* (without), *gune, gyn-* (woman), and *ophelos* (advantage, help).

Although sex was not all-important to Neil, it was important enough for him to break off his engagement to Belinda when he discovered her **agynophelimity.**

aidocratia (ī-dō-cra-tē-ə): the sexual desire aroused in a man by the bashfulness of a girl; also the additional sexual potency in males stimulated by female bashfulness. Derived from Greek *aidos* (modesty, shame) and *kratos* (power, strength).

Because Raymond is a highly confident man who likes to play the role of protector, his friends were hardly surprised that, the more bashful women were around him, the more pronounced his **aidocratia** *would be.*

aidomania (ī-dō-MĀN-ē-ə): abnormal sexual craving for female genitalia. Derived from Greek *aidoion* (female genitalia) and *mania* (madness, craving).

When we discovered that James had experienced sexual relations with not only every high school cheerleader but also all their mothers, we knew that his **aidomania** *had completely destroyed his reason.*

aischrolatreia (īs-krō-lə-TRĪ-ə): worship of filth or obscenity. Derived from Greek *aischros* (shameful, ugly) and *-latres* (worship).

Hustler magazine shows that appealing to **aischrolatreia** *can be highly profitable.*

aischrology (īs-KROL-ə-jē): "dirty" words or language. Derived from Greek *aischros* (shameful, ugly) and *-logy* (discourse, study).

Our high school principal told us that **aischrology** *is unacceptable, even in the locker room.*

algolagnia (*ălgō*-LAG-nē-ə): a sexual condition in which inflicting pain or suffering pain produces sexual gratification or increases sexual excitement. Derived from Greek *algos* (pain) and *lagneia* (lust).

When we saw Mookie and Rosie enter their bedroom with a lighted candle, a bucket of ice, and a chip clip but no chips, we suspected them of engaging in **algolagnia.**

algolagnist (älgō-LAG-nist): a person who derives sexual pleasure from either inflicting pain, suffering pain, or both. Derived from Greek *algos* (pain) and *lagneia* (lust).

Because Michael was an **algolagnist,** *he enjoyed introducing women to his dungeon.*

algophilia (älgō-FIL-ē-ə): arousal from experiencing pain. Derived from Greek *algos* (pain) and *philia* (attachment, attraction).

*When we heard Geraldo tell us that the spanking he received from his wife produced a "good kind of pain," we learned about his **algophilia**.*

algorgasmia (älgor-GAZ-mē-ə): painful orgasm in the male. Derived from Latin *algor* (coldness) and Greek *orgasmos* (a swelling).

*When Bill Clinton's vice president ran for the presidency in 2000, he presented himself as sexually vital and almost incapable of **algorgasmia**.*

algorsenia (älgor-SĒN-ē-ə): lack of sexual desire in males. Derived from Latin *algor* (coldness) and Greek *arrhen* (male).

*When the 105-year-old man rebuffed the prostitute by telling her that he was no longer interested in sex, she told him that she could cure him of his **algorsenia**.*

algoterpsia (älgə/gō-TERP-sē-ə): a moral sternness demanding that any pleasure, especially sexual, be followed by punishment, particularly the infliction of pain. Derived from Greek *algos* (pain) and *terpsis* (enjoyment).

*Pamela's sadistic tendencies perfectly complemented Raymond's **algoterpsia**, as when she would slap him after their sexual encounters, and chide him for his naughtiness.*

aliphineur (al-ə-fə-NUR): a man skilled at applying ointments on people to induce sexual excitement. Derived from Greek *aleiphein* (to anoint).

*A crude man but a talented **aliphineur**, Sean used to say, "Oil 'em before you despoil 'em."*

allantotribism (ə-lan-tō-TRIB-izəm): female masturbation in which a sausage is used. Derived from the Greek *allas* (sausage) and *tribein* (to rub).

*After seeing a porn movie depicting **allantotribism**, the young man quickly lost his appetite for the cookout.*

alleloknismus (al-ə-lō-NIZ-məs): a form of masturbation, often practiced by children, in which the participants tickle one anothers' sexual organs. Derived from Greek *allelon* (one another) and *knismos* (tickling).

*About ninety-eight percent of people who do not think oral sex qualifies as sex believe that **alleloknismus** is simply playful tickling.*

alloandrism (al-lō-AN-driz-əm): a woman's imagining her male sexual partner is someone else whom she finds more desirable. Derived from Greek *allos* (other) and *aner, andr-* (man). (*See also* **allorgasmia**.)

*Marie, who liked to imagine that Otis was her idol, Richard Simmons, when Marie and Otis would make love, hoped that Otis would never discover her **alloandrism**.*

alloerasty (al-lō-i-RAS-tē): use of nudity of a third party to arouse one's sexual partner. Derived from Greek *allolos* (different) and *erastes* (lover).
*The couple would visit bars to pick up some attractive stranger so that Ray could indulge Sheryl's **alloerasty**.*

allogynia (allō-JIN/GĪN-ē-ə): a man's imagining his female sexual partner to be a different and more desirable one. Derived from Greek *allos* (another) and *gune, gyn-* (woman).
*Monty would engage in **allogynia** when he would make love with Doris, whom he imagined to be his idol, actress Agnes Morehead.*

alloiophilia (al-loiō-FIL-ē-ə): an old term for "heterosexuality." Derived from Greek *allolos* (different) and *philia* (attachment, attraction).
*The evangelist asserted that God showed a distinct preference for **alloiophlia** in having created Adam and Eve, and not Adam and Steve.*

allomulcia (al-lō-MUL-sē-ə): the desire to caress or fondle a woman in the presence of another woman. Derived from Greek *allos* (other) and Latin *mulceo* (to stroke).
*Because Jason enjoyed having sex with women, engaging in exhibitionism, and making women jealous, his **allomulcia** made sense.*

allopellia (al-lō-PEL-ē-ə): the condition of having an orgasm from watching others make love. Derived from Greek *allos* (other) and Latin *pello* (to expel).
*Because of his capacity for **allopellia**, Brutus would content himself to watch his girlfriend commingle with her sailor-suitor.*

allorgasmia (al-lor-GAZ-mē-ə): arousal from fantasizing about someone other than one's partner. Derived from Greek *allolos* (different), *orgasmos* (swelling, excitement), and *-ia* (condition).
*Bev enjoyed sex with Ray because of the **allorgasmia** produced from fantasizing about Fabio.*

allovalent (al-ə-VĀ-lənt): a male's ability to have sex with only women other than his wife. Derived from Greek *allos* (other) and Latin *valere* (to be strong). (*See also* **heterovalent**.)
*The **allovalent** aristocrat used to joke that sex was important to him—so long as it is not with his wife.*

altocalciphilia (al-tō-kal-si-FIL-ē-ə): a special attraction to females in high heels. Derived from Latin *altus* (high), Latin *calcis* (heel), and Greek *philia* (attachment, attraction).
*The executive liked to indulge in **altocalciphilia** and masochism by persuading women to dig their high heels into his chest.*

alvinolagnia (al-vin-ō-LAG-nē-ə): arousal from a stomach; stomach fetish. Derived from Latin *alvus* (belly or abdomen) and Greek *lagneia* (lust).
*Britney's stomach is attractive enough to appeal to the **alvinolagnia** of countless males.*

alvojaction (al-vō-JAK-shən): a bodily movement, as in burlesque shows, in which a woman causes her abdomen to perform provocative gyrations. Derived from Latin *alvus* (belly or abdomen) and *jactare* (to thrust or throw).
*After seeing the young woman's **alvojaction** on the dance floor, the nun informed her that she was at a cotillion, not a Madonna concert.*

amatorculist (am-ə-TOR-ku-list): a pitiful or insignificant lover. Derived from Latin *amo* (to love), *-cule* (small), *-ist* (one who).
*The judge defended his marital infidelity by asserting that oral sex with an **amatorculist** barely violates marital vows.*

amatory dextrality (AM-ə-*tor*-ē dek-STRAL-i-tē): the faculty for effectively expressing one's affection for a member of the opposite sex. Derived from Latin *amo* (to love) and *dextralis* (on the right side).
*The original Casanova was an eighteenth-century man who revealed his **amatory dextrality** in his actions and in his* Memoirs.

amatory mancinism (AM-ə-*tor*-ē MAN-(t)sə-nizəm): awkwardness, especially in males, in expressing affection for members of the opposite sex. Derived from Latin *amo* (to love) and Italian *mancinismo*, from *mancino* (left-handed).
When Fielding Mellish (Woody Allen) asks his coworkers in the movie Bananas *whether he looks like the kind of guy who would have trouble in bed, their expressions reveal their belief in his **amatory mancinism**.*

amatripsis (am-ə-TRIP-sis): a form of female masturbation in which the labia majora are rubbed against each other. Derived from Greek *ama* (together) and *tripsis* (rubbing).
*Ginger said that she would practice **amatripsis** because she was the only person on the island whom she found attractive.*

amaurophilia (ə-märō-FIL-ē-ə): the tendency for people to be aroused by sexual partners unable to see them, not because of blindness but because one or both partners are blindfolded, or having sex in the dark. Derived from the Greek *amauros* (dark, dim) and *philia* (attachment, attraction).

*Because Barney always insisted on turning out the lights before he and Thelma Lou made love, she wondered whether he had **amaurophilia**.*

ambibiosis (am-bē-BĪ-ō-sis): the nonsexual living together of a gay person with a heterosexual member of the opposite sex. Derived from Latin *ambo* (both), Greek *bios* (life), and *-osis* (a condition).

Because the TV show Three's Company *focused on the adventures of Jack Tripper (John Ritter), who pretended to be gay, and his two heteosexual female roommates, the show focused on a simulated **ambibiosis**.*

ambisexual (am-bi-SEK-shoo-əl): bisexual person. Derived from Latin *ambo* (both) and Latin *sexus* (sex).

*The term "switch-hitter" is slang for an "**ambisexual**."*

amblyrosis (am-bli-RŌ-sis): the dulling of sexual appetite, as over time or through excessive indulgence. Derived from Greek *amblys* (dull) and *eros* (sexual desire).

*The ex-politician asserted that his political adversaries hated him not so much for his political views as for his vitality and possible immunity to **amblyrosis**.*

ambosexual (*am*-bō/bə-SEK-shoo-əl): exhibiting or constituting sexual traits common to both sexes. Derived from Latin *ambo* (both) and *sexus* (sex).

*Axillary or armpit hair is an **ambosexual** characteristic.*

amomaxia (amō-MAKS-ē-ə): lovemaking or necking in a parked car, usually in a lovers' lane. Derived from the Latin *amo* (to love) and Greek *amaxa* (wagon).

*When the basketball player engaged in the most vigorous form of **amomaxia** in the Pinto, he sprained his back.*

amphigenesis (am-phi-JEN-i-sis): a form of sexuality in which a predominantly homosexual person is able to have sexual relations with members of the opposite sex; also known as "amphigenic inversion," in contradistinction to "absolute inversion" (complete homosexuality). Derived from Greek *ampho* (both) and *gignesthai* (to be born).

*Spike described Mookie's relationship with Tamara as reflecting "lukewarm heterosexuality, **amphigenesis**."*

amphiphilia (am-phi-FIL-ē-ə): ability to love persons of either sex; bisexuality. Derived from Greek *ampho* (both) and *philia* (attachment, attraction).

The historian asserted that, while some ancient Greeks were exclusively homosexual in their behavior, more Greeks experienced amphiphilia than exclusive homosexuality.

amplexia (am-PLEKS-ē-ə): a sexual position in which a woman lies supine and embraces the loins of the man with her legs. (*See* **Oceanic position**.) Derived from Latin *amplexus* (embrace).

When the young executive and his secretary were caught by his wife in a position of amplexia, the executive feebly remarked, "This isn't what it looks like."

amulierosis (ə-*mū*-lē-i-RŌS-is): "mental disorder" resulting from not associating or having intercourse with women. Derived from Greek *a* (without) and Latin *mulier* (woman) and *-osis* (Greek-derived noun suffix for condition, process, or action).

When the sexologist asserted that one of the main factors promoting murders by serial killers is amulierosis, we knew that he was oversimplifying the killers' psyches.

amychesis (am-i-KĒ-sis): an expression of sexual heat in which an excited woman scratches her male companion during sex, typically to release tension of the libido. Derived from Greek *amyktikos* (scratching).

When Chester's mother asked him about the source of the marks left by his girlfriend's amychesis, he replied that the marks were created by his cat.

anaclitism (an-ə-KLIT-izəm): arousal by adults from activities or objects appropriate for children. Derived from Greek *anaklinein* (to lean upon) and *-ismos* (stuff).

Bill's habit of having his wife bathe him, spank him, and punish him were all aspects of his anaclitism.

anaphrodisiac (a-na-frə-DIZ-ē-ak): a substance, commonly a medicine, calming or reducing sexual desire. Derived from Greek *a-, an-* (without) and *aphrodisia* (sexual pleasures, related to *Aphrodite*, goddess of love).

Even if someone could find an effective anaphrodisiac for Bill, no one can make him take a substance that could quell his voracious sexual appetite.

anapocrisis (an-ə-POK-ri-sis): lack of response from a female sexual partner. Derived from Greek *a-, an-* (without) and *apokrisis* (answer).

*Fred was so angry with Ethel's **anapocrisis** that he told her that having sex with her was like having sex with a corpse. In response, she said, "You should know."*

androgyny (an-DROJ-ə-nē): originally, the condition of having a sexually ambiguous body build that is neither distinctly masculine nor distinctly feminine. Now the term may refer to the exhibition of characteristics in physical appearance, dress, or behavior that suggest both sexes. Derived from Greek *aner, andr-* (man) and *gune, -gyn* (woman).

*The facial features of actor Christopher Walken suggest **androgyny**.*

andromania (an-drō-MĀN-ē-ə): little-used term for "nymphomania," an "uncontrollable" desire in women for sex with men. Derived from Greek *aner, andr-* (man) and *mania* (madness, craving).

*The psychiatrist stated that, although he has not met the young woman under discussion, it is likely any woman who feels the need to have sex with a dozen men within one hour is suffering from **andromania**.*

andromimetophilia (an-drō-mi-me-tō-FIL-ē-ə): term coined by author John Money, author of *Lovemaps*, to refer to arousal from female imitation of males, as in dress. Derived from Greek *aner, andr-* (man), *mimesis* (mimicry), and *philia* (attachment, attraction).

*Jason likes women who affect the "Annie Hall look" because of his **andromimetophilia**.*

androphilist (an-DROF-ə-list): a female especially fond of males. Derived from Greek *aner, andr-* (man), *philein* (to love), and *-ist* (suffix ending for "one who").

*Al told reporters that his wife is an **androphilist** whose husband fully satisfies her appetites.*

androphobia (an-drō-FŌB-ē-ə): strong fear or dislike of men by a woman. Derived from Greek *aner, andr-* (man) and *phobos* (fear).

*The lesbian submitted that, although she is not sexually attracted to men, she likes them as friends, and is in no sense affected by **androphobia**.*

androsodomy (an-drō-SOD-ə-mē): anal sex with a male partner. Derived from the Greek *aner, andr-* (men) and the Latin *sodoma* (Sodom).

*The gay comedian said that **androsodomy** involves knowing somebody at bottom.*

androzoon (an-drō-ZŌ-on): a male animal trained to perform sexual intercourse with a woman. Derived from Greek *andr-* (man) and *zoon* (animal).

*When Jackie told us that her dog had appeared in some exciting movies with her, we had no idea that she was alluding to an **androzoon**.*

anililagnia (an-ī-li-LAG-nē-ə): arousal from an older female. Derived from Latin *anilis* (from *anus*, old woman) and Greek *lagneia* (lust).

*Although Reggie was only thirty-five, he would go to restaurants during "Senior Citizen Day" to meet people to try to indulge his **anililagnia**.*

anisomastia (ə/a-nī-sə-MAS-tē-ə): condition of one breast's being larger than the other. Derived from Greek *anisos* (unequal), *mastos* (breast), and *-ia* (condition of).

*Because Margaret skillfully stuffed her right bra cup with material to fill it up, people did not notice her **anisomastia**.*

anolinguist (ano-LING-guist): someone who licks an anus. Derived from Latin *ānus* (ring, anus), *lingere* (to lick), and *-ist* (suffix meaning "one who").

*When June discovered that Ward was an **anolinguist**, she made him the butt of her jokes.*

anomeatia (anō-mē-AT-ē-ə): anal intercourse with a female. Derived from Latin *ano-* (anus), *meatus* (passage, past participle of *meare*, "to go"), and *-ia* (condition).

***Anomeatia** is fairly common in heterosexual pornography, though not so common as vaginal intercourse.*

anophelimity (ə-nə-fə-LIM-i-tē): inability of men sexually to satisfy their partners. Derived from Greek *a-* (without) and *ophelimos* (useful, helpful).

*Karen left Frank because his **anophelimity** frustrated her.*

anophelophobia (ə-nə-fə-lō-FŌ-bē-ə): a man's morbid fear of hurting his female partner through sexual intercourse. Derived from the Greek *anopheles* (hurtful, useless) and *phobos* (fear).

*The newly married man became impotent because of his **anophelophobia**.*

anophelorastia (ə-nə-fə-lō-RAS-tē-ə): the tendency to be aroused from defilement, as when people pollute, destroy, or violate a fetish object, or sex partner, or themselves. Some men, for example, are sexually aroused by cutting, or throwing ink onto, the clothes of a female passerby. Other men are aroused by urinating on women. Derived from Greek *anopheles* (hurtful, useless) and *erastes* (lover).

> *We did not learn about Roger's **anophelorastia** until we saw him trying to urinate on female passersby.*

anophile (an-ō-FĪL): a male sexually attracted to elderly women. Derived from Latin *anus* (old woman) and Greek *philein* (to love).

> *Although Lamont was only fifteen, he was an **anophile** who sought women at least fifty years his senior.*

anophilemia (an-ō-fi-LĒM-ē-ə): the act of kissing an anus. Derived from Latin *ano-* (anus), Greek *phileo* (to kiss), and *-ia* (state, condition).

> *Speaking sarcastically, Betty said that she engages in **anophilemia** whenever she kisses Barney.*

anophilous (ə-NOF-i-ləs): being especially attracted to the anus. Derived from Latin *ānus* (anus) and Greek *philein* (to love).

> *When asked about the objects of his devotion, Gomez said that he is **anophilous**.*

anorast (AN-ə-RAST): a male who anally penetrates a female. Derived from Latin *ānus* (anus) and Greek *erastes* (lover).

> *While many men have experienced peno-vaginal intercourse, fewer men are **anorasts**.*

apandria (span-drē-ə): an aversion to males. Derived from Greek *apo-* (away from, separate) and *aner, andr-* (man).

> *The lesbian explained that while lesbians are sexually interested in women, they usually do not have **apandria**.*

apellous (APEL-əs): pertaining to a circumcised penis. Derived from Greek *a-* (without) and Latin *pellis* (hide, leather cover).

> *The Israeli woman asked the American whom she met at the bar whether he was **apellous**.*

aphallatosis (*ā*-fal-lə-TŌ-sis): "mental disorder" resulting from unsatisfactory sex life. Derived from Greek *a-* (without), *phallos* (penis), and *-osis* (noun suffix for designating some condition, action, or process).

> *The psychiatrist asserted that not everyone who has an unsatisfactory sex life develops **aphallatosis**.*

aphrodisiac (a-frō-DIZ-ē-ak): a chemical or other substance that is supposed to increase sexual desire or stamina. The term comes from Greek *aphrodisia* (sexual pleasures).

*In ancient Rome, it is reported that some people used to drink the blood of slain gladiators because it was thought the blood could function as an **aphrodisiac**.*

apistia (ə-PIS-tē-ə): adultery. Derived from the Greek *a-* (without), *pistis* (faith), and *-ia* (condition).

*The discovery of former senator Gary Hart's **apistia** ruined his chances of becoming president.*

apodyopsis (ap-ə-dī-OP-sis): the habit of mentally undressing a woman. Derived from Greek *apodyo* (undress) and *opsis* (sight, vision).

*The high school student was staring at the girl with such longing intensity that she could sense his **apodyopsis**.*

apotemnophilia (a-po-*tim*-nō-FIL-ē-ə): arousal from fantasizing about losing a limb, or having a body part surgically removed. Derived from Greek *apo-* (away from, separate), *temno* (to cut), and *philia* (attachment, attraction).

*Most people who have **apotemnophilia** fantasize about losing a limb when they masturbate, but do not purposely injure themselves to increase their chances of losing a limb.*

arachnephilia (a-rak-nə-FIL-ē-ə): the tendency to be sexually aroused by spiders. Derived from Greek *arachne* (spider) and *philia* (attachment, attraction).

*When I learned of my girlfriend's **arachnephilia**, I told her that we should avoid black widows, lest we should violate the guidelines for safe sex.*

arrhenogynia (ar-ən-ō-GIN/jin-ē-ə): the condition of a female who has a masculine figure, face, or carriage. Derived from the Greek *arrhen* (male) and *gune, gyn-* (woman).

*Some people insist that, although the actress Jamie Lee Curtis has an attractive face, it suggests **arrhenogynia**.*

arrhenothigmophilous (ar-ən-ō-thig-MOF-il-əs): characterized by the desire (hardly unusual) to see a man touching a woman's sexual parts. Derived from Greek *arrhen* (male), *thigma* (touch), and *philein* (to love).

*After the feminist called a young rock star who collected pornography "brazenly **arrhenothigmophilous**," he replied that he would just have to live with that label.*

arsenosadism (är-sə-nō-SĀ-diz-əm): sexual pleasure from inflicting cruelty on males. Derived from Greek *arrhen* (male) and *sadism* (from Marquis de Sade [1740–1814], an aristocratic Parisian whose life and writings focused on sexual cruelty).
> *Donald felt strangely attracted to women whose* **arsenosadism** *caused them to mistreat him.*

arsometry (är-SOM-i-trē): anal sex. Derived from *arse* (of which "ass" is a variant) and Greek *metreo* (to measure).
> *Most women prefer "conventional" intercourse to* **arsometry***.*

artamesia (är-tə-MĒ-zhə): a state experienced by women of being left sexually unsatisfied, as if hanging in midair because of a man's premature orgasm. Derived from Greek *artao* (to hang), *mesos* (middle), and *-ia* (condition).
> *Rebecca asked Isaac to take his time in bed because she was getting tired of experiencing* **artamesia***.*

asthenolagnia (as-*thenō*-LAG-nē-ə): arousal from being humiliated, as from wearing a collar, receiving insults, or having one's genitals shaved. Derived from Greek *astheneia* (weakness) and *lagneia* (lust).
> *When Mike would have sex with Carol, he would appeal to her* **asthenolagnia** *by calling her a "horny slut."*

aterpsia (ə-TURP-sē-ə): the belief that sexual intercourse must be engaged in only for the sake of procreation and not for pleasure, often associated with religion, such as Roman Catholicism. Derived from Greek *a-* (without) and *terpsis* (enjoyment).
> *The* **aterpsia** *of the Roman Catholic church, whose teachings Bill had absorbed as a child, caused him to feel guilty whenever he made love to his infertile wife.*

autagonistophilia (ôt-ə-go/gə-nis-tō-FIL-ē-ə): the tendency to be aroused by being on stage or performing for someone holding a camera. Derived from Greek *autos* (self), *agonistes* (one engaged in a struggle, including a literary character or an actor), and *philia* (attachment, attraction).
> *We discovered Amber's* **autagonistophilia** *when she told us that she was aroused by arousing others.*

autocunnilingus (ôt-ō-kun-ə-LING-gəs): a woman's performing oral sex on her own vulva. Derived from Greek *autos* (self), Latin *cunnus* (vulva), and Latin *lingere* (to lick).

*The controversial rock star asserted that she learned gymnastics to become capable of performing **autocunnilingus**.*

autoerotic asphyxia: a dangerous sexual practice engaged in principally by adolescent males who try to heighten the pleasure of masturbation by near-asphyxiation. Derived from Greek *autos* (self), *eros* (sexual love), *a-* (without), and *sphyzein* (to throb). The FBI has estimated that hundreds of accidental deaths (especially those involving hanging) are self-inflicted but often misdiagnosed as suicides or homicides.

*The eccentric coroner confided in us that, whenever young men die of **autoerotic asphyxia**, they are disproving the dangerous myth that masturbation is safe sex. "We are all diminished," he said, "when we allow reckless masturbators to walk the streets with impunity."*

autofellatio (ôt-ō-fə-LĀ-shē-ō): performing oral sex on one's own penis. Derived from Greek *autos* (self) and Latin *fellare* (to suck).

*When Jeff's mother caught him performing **autofellatio**, he told her that he was at least having sex with someone he loved.*

autofetishism: a form of narcissism in which one becomes sexually obsessed with one's own body. Derived from Greek *autos* (self) and Latin *facticius* (artificial).

*Rush's **autofetishism** became so ridiculous that he put up wallpaper containing pictures of his naked body, and would masturbate while watching a video of himself masturbating.*

automasochism: arousal from inflicting pain on oneself. Derived from Greek *autos* (self) and the name of the nineteenth-century German novelist Leopold von Sacher-Masoch, who wrote about and exemplified the behavior and who, like Marquis de Sade, was committed to an asylum.

*When Brian entered his bedroom by himself with a lighted candle and a bowl of ice, we did not realize that he was planning to indulge his **automasochism**.*

automysophilia (ôt-ō-*mī*-se-FIL-ē-ə): arousal from being dirtied or defiled. Derived from Greek *autos* (self), *mysos* (dirt, uncleanness), and *phobos* (fear).

*We thought that Howard's **automysophilia** might explain his masturbating while rolling in the mud and horse manure.*

autonecrophilia (ôt-ō-*ne-krō*-FIL-ē-ə): sexual pleasure derived from imagining oneself as a corpse. Derived from Greek *autos* (self), *nekros* (corpse), and *philia* (attachment, attraction).

Dick was stunned to learn that Jane's sexual passivity was due to
autonecrophilia.

autonepiophilia (ôt-ō-*ne*-pē-ə-FIL-ē-ə): arousal from playing the role of an infant, especially when using objects or engaging in acts associated with childhood. Derived from Greek *autos* (self), *nepios* (infant), and *philia* (attachment, attraction).
*We could not believe that Max, a powerful executive, would ask his wife to diaper him and to tuck him in bed, because at work he would never show signs of **autonepiophilia**.*

autopederasty (ôt-ō-pe-də-RAS-tē): the act of performing anal intercourse on oneself. Derived from Greek *autos* (self) and *paiderastes* (lover of boys).
*The controversial rock star asserted that the only time he has sex without a condom occurs when he engages in **autopederasty**.*

autopedophilia (ôt-ō-pe-dō-FIL-ē-ə): sexual arousal from imagining oneself as a child and from being treated as a child during sex. Derived from Greek *autos* (self), *paidos* (child), and *philia* (attachment, attraction).
*After we discovered Michael's **autopedophilia**, his collection of Pee Wee Herman dolls and posters took on an even stranger meaning.*

autoscopophilia (ôt-ō-skōp-ō-FIL-ē-ə): sexual arousal from looking at one's own body, especially one's genitalia. Derived from Greek *autos* (self), *skopein* (to view), and *philia* (attachment, attraction).
*Laura's **autoscopophilia** became so strong that she had mirrors in every room.*

avestaphrenia (ə/a-*ves-tə*-FRĒN-ē-ə): female dysphoria resulting from "not having a thing to wear." Derived from Greek *a-* (without), Latin *vestimenti* (clothes), and Greek *phren* (mind).
*Ricky felt driven to buy Lucy a whole new wardrobe to alleviate her **avestaphrenia**.*

avirgynia (avur-JIN/GĪN-ē-ə): the absence of sexual relations between a man and his wife. Derived from Greek *a-* (without), Latin *vir* (man), and Greek *gune, gyn-* (woman).
*Often when husbands engage in what is sometimes called "serial promiscuity," they are experiencing **avirgynia** at home.*

avisodomy (a-vi-SOD-ə-mē): sexual intercourse between a human male and a bird. Derived from Latin *avis* (bird) and *sodoma* (Sodom).

*The politician feared that the revelation of his **avisodomy** might alienate some voters, especially religious members of the Audobon Society.*

axillism (ak-si-LIZ(ə)m): the use of the armpit for sex, especially in male penetration of females. Derived from Latin *axilla* (armpit).

*After the young man returned to the United States from Europe, where women commonly have armpit hair, he wanted to introduce his girlfriend to **axillism**.*

B

balanic (bə-LANIK): relating to the glans penis (head) or clitoris. Derived from Greek *balanos* (acorn, head of the male organ).

*In the locker room the boys would sometimes tease one another when drawing **balanic** comparisons.*

balanotage (bal-in-ə-TÔZH): playful manipulation of the glans penis (the head of the penis), often part of foreplay. Derived from Greek *balanos* (acorn, head of male organ) and French *barboter* (to dabble, to splash about, or play).

*The former governor thought that he was doing secretaries he hardly knew a great favor by inviting them for **balanotage**.*

basculocolpia (bas-kū-lə-KÔL-pē-e): provocative swaying of the breasts. Derived from Greek *basculer* (to swing or sway) and *kolpos* (breast, womb, vagina).

*The exercise instructor liked to assign jumping jacks to women so that he could watch **basculocolpia**.*

basculophilia (bas-kū-lə-FIL-ē-e): a sexual attraction to being rocked or swayed; thought by some theorists to be a yearning for prenatal uterine swaying. Derived from Greek *basculer* (to swing or sway) and *philia* (attachment, attraction).

*Ever since Ralph bought Alice three rocking chairs for their bedroom and promised to rock her to the moon, their neighbor Ed suspected that Alice had **basculophilia**.*

basial (BĀZ-ē-əl): pertaining to kissing. Derived from Latin *basium* (kiss).

*The principal reminded the young woman and her boyfriend that the hallways were not designed for **basial** activity.*

basorexia (bā/ba-sō-REKS-ē-e): a strong craving for kissing. Derived from Latin *basium* (a kiss) and Latin/Greek *orexis* (desire, appetite).
Archie, a true romantic, loved to kiss, but his **basorexia** *was particularly stimulated by Mehitabel, especially when she would lick her lips.*

basorgasmus (bā/ba-sor-GAZ-mus): sexual orgasm produced by kissing. Derived from Latin *basium* (a kiss) and Greek *orgasmos* (swelling).
So intense were her feelings for her boyfriend that Maria would experience **basorgasmus** *while necking.*

basorthosis (bā/ba-sor-THŌ-sis): an erection caused by kissing. Derived from Latin *basium* (a kiss) and Greek *orthosis* (a straightening).
When Ginger and her sister Amber both kissed Mr. Thomas, he had to excuse himself because of his embarrassing **basorthosis**.

bathycolpian (ba-thi-KŌL-pē-ən): have deep bosoms. Derived from Greek *bathys-* (deep) and *kolpos* (breast, womb, vagina).
Bathycolpian *women get men's attention, especially when the women wear tight blouses.*

bedswerver: archaic term for "adulterer."
An inveterate **bedswerver**, *the famous actor was constantly unfaithful to his wife.*

benign orgasmic cephalgia (bi-NĪN or-GAZ-mik sə-FAL-jē(ə)): a headache associated only with orgasm, affecting both sides of the head and lasting about an hour or longer. It affects more men than women. Derived from Latin *benignus* (kind, friendly), Greek *orgasmos* (swelling), and Greek *kephale* (head).

bestiality (*bes*-chē-AL-i-tē): sex between a human being and an animal. Derived from Latin *bestia* (beast).
The sexologist asserted that people who engage in bestiality often choose dogs or sheep for the objects of their libido.

biastophilia (bī-as-tō-FIL-ē-e): attraction to, or arousal from, sexually assaulting an unwilling victim. Derived from Greek *biastos* (violent) and *philia* (attachment, attraction).
Serial rapists in prison soon discover that their **biastophilia** *is greeted with contempt and often violence among other prisoners.*

bigynist (bī-JI-nist): a man involved in a threesome with two women. Derived from Latin *bi-* (two), Greek *gune, gyn-* (woman), *-ist* (one who).

*The young man starred in pornographic movies because he enjoyed being a **bigynist**, and was seldom satisfied with only one woman at a time.*

birthday party: euphemism for "orgy."
*We did not realize that Francis's so-called **birthday party** was an orgy until we saw Lucille and everyone else in their birthday suits.*

bivirist (bī-VĒR-ist): a woman who is involved in a threesome with two men. Derived from Latin *bi-* (two), *vir* (man), and *-ist* (one who).
__Bivirists__ are commonly needed in pornographic movies, where women are often expected to have sex with two men at a time.

blastolagnia (blas-tō-LAG-nē-e): arousal from young females. Derived from Greek *blastos* (bud) and *lagneia* (lust).
*A middle-aged midwestern politician who recklessly displays his **blastolagnia** with an eighteen-year-old woman can usually expect to need another job.*

body-work therapist: a sexual surrogate who teaches social and sexual skills by serving as a partner for the client/patient and assisting the person in carrying out the clinician's suggestions.
*When we heard that Billy was going to a **body-work therapist**, we thought that he was visiting a masseuse, not a sexual surrogate.*

botulinonia (bôch-ə-li-NŌ-nē-e): a form of female masturbation in which a sausage, often lubricated and at times heated, is introduced into the vagina. Derived from Latin *botulus* (sausage) and Greek *koinonia* (sexual intercourse).
*Because of her daughter's proclivity for **botulinonia**, Mary would buy only sausages in patties and never link-shaped sausages.*

boustrophate (boō-strə-FĀT): to behave clumsily in lovemaking. Derived from Greek *bous* (ox) and *strepho* (to turn).
*Millie said that although she wanted a lover as suave as James Bond, she ended up with Jerry, a maladroit, **boustrophating** nerd, incapable of getting out of a telephone booth with four doors.*

brachiophilous (*bra*-kē-ÔF-i-ləs): especially attracted to a person's arms, a word applied particularly to males. Derived from Latin *brachium* (arm, forearm) and *philein* (to love).
*While most men are especially attracted to women's faces, breasts, legs, or buttocks, some men are **brachiophilous** and become excited by sleeveless women.*

brachioproctic eroticism (*bra*-kē-ō-PROK-tik): a form of (anal) fisting in which part of the arm of one partner enters the anus of the other partner. Derived from Latin *brachium* (arm, forearm), Greek *proktos* (anus), and *erotikos* (sexual love).

*In his lecture on safe sex, the physician warned that **brachioproctic eroticism** can easily cause injury.*

brachycraspedonia (*bra*-kē-craz-pe-DŌN-ē-ə): the pleasure men experience from watching women in miniskirts. Derived from Greek *brachys* (short), *kraspedon* (hem, border), and *hedone* (pleasure).

*When we saw Dash salivating when ogling Elly in her miniskirt, we knew that he was overcome by **brachycraspedonia**.*

brachycubia (*bra*-kē-KŪB-ē-ə): a short or fast form of intercourse. Derived from Greek *brachy-* (short) and Latin *cubare* (to lie down).

*Reportedly, President Kennedy said that lovemaking, including **brachycubia**, was necessary at least every few days for him to prevent headaches.*

brachyphallia (*bra*-kē-FAL-ē-ə): the condition of having a short penis. Derived from Greek *brachy-* (short) and *phallos* (penis).

*Rightly or wrongly, many Republicans assert that former President Clinton's **brachyphallia** has been established by legal testimony.*

bradycontia (*brad*-i-KONT-ē-ə): in sexual intercourse, a slowing of male ejaculation; as happens because of older age. Derived from Greek *brady-* (slow) and *anakontizo* (to spurt out).

*Della complained that Perry's **bradycontia** meant that she would fall asleep from boredom before he could achieve orgasm.*

bradycubia (*brad*-i-KŪB-ē-ə): the male practice of slowly penetrating his partner's vagina or anus, usually at the beginning of the encounter. Derived from the Greek *brady-* (slow) and Latin *cubare* (to lie down).

*The politician defended himself against the charge that he had slept with his secretary at work by saying that he did not have time to lie down to rest, much less to perform **bradycubia** with an employee.*

bradyorthosis (*brad*-i-or-THŌ-sis): the condition in which the penis is slow in developing a complete erection. Derived from Greek *brady-* (slow) and *orthosis* (a straightening).

*The call girl asserted that, because time is money, she does not have time to serve several clients with **bradyorthosis**.*

buccal intercourse (BUK-əl IN-tər-kors): a term occasionally used for oral-genital sex. Derived from Latin *bucca* (cheek) and *intercurrere* (to mingle with).

Relying on the common law understanding of adultery, in which vaginal penetration by the male is required, the lawyer argued that his client's passive status in **buccal intercourse** *disqualifies as adultery.*

buccal onanism (BUK-əl ō-nə-NIZ-əm): oral sex. Derived from Latin *bucca* (cheek) and *onanism* (Onan, a biblical figure associated with *coitus interruptus*).

The Republican senator told members of the PTA that, because a Republican now occupies the White House, parents will no longer have to explain **buccal onanism** *to seven-year-old children, and no longer have to explain how the Oval Office was once briefly called the "Oral Office."*

buggery (BUG-ə-rē): a legal and colloquial term for anal sex. Derived from the medieval Latin *Bulgarus* because Bulgarian heretics (religious nonconformists) were once reputed by their enemies to practice anal sex.

***Buggery** and almost all other sexual acts are illegal in the commonwealth of Virginia.*

bulbourethral (*bul*-bō-yoo-RĒ-thrəl): pertaining to the bulb of the penis. Derived from Latin *bulbus* (bulb, onion) and Greek *ourein* (to urinate).

"This impeachment is not about sex but about truth, especially the truth about President Clinton's **bulbourethral** *behavior," said the Republican representative.*

C

cacavalence (ka-ka-VĀ-ləns): impotence resulting from a feeling of guilt. Derived from Greek *kakon* (guilt), Latin *a-* (not), and Latin *valere* (to be strong).

As soon as Friedrich thought about the pain that knowledge of his infidelity could cause his wife, he experienced **cacavalence,** *leading him to jump out of the hotel bed, and to call off his tryst with Matilda.*

cacocallia (*kak*-ō-KAL-ē-ə): the condition of being both ugly and sexually attractive. Derived from Greek *kakos* (bad) and *kallos* (beauty).

Many men find Sandra Bernhardt sexually attractive, but some men consider her appeal to be due to **cacocallia.**

cacophallic (*kak*-ō-FAL-ik): having a sexually inadequate phallus, as one that is insufficiently large or erect. Derived from Greek *kakos* (bad) and *phallos* (penis).

> *When the prostitute told the **cacophallic** man that she never wanted to see him or his "ugly nub," he was devastated.*

cagamosis (kag-ə-MŌ-sis): an unhappy marriage. Derived from Greek *kakos* (bad) and *gamos* (marriage).

> *The divorce lawyer said that, while a **cagamosis** is unpleasant for the couple involved, it often leads to divorce, which is good for him.*

calliandrus (kal-lē-AN-drus): a handsome male with a stimulating penis. Derived from Greek *kallos* (beauty) and *andrus* (man as a male).

> *Both Thelma Lou and her gay friend Howard were looking for some wealthy **calliandrus** who could satisfy their every wish.*

callibombe (*KAL*-lē-bom): the state or condition of having attractive anatomical curves, including breasts, buttocks, and hips. Derived from Greek *kallos* (beauty) and French *bombe* (rounded or bulging).

> *Rosie's body fits many people's standards for feminine beauty, since her physical beauty is due to her **callibombe**.*

callicacia (*kal*-li-KĀ-she): a state of mind produced by love or passion in which even what most people would consider bad or ugly in one's sexual partner seems appropriate and beautiful. Derived from Greek *kallos* (beauty) and Latin *caecus* (blind).

> *In her **callicacia** her husband's asymmetrical face seemed fitting, even attractive.*

callicolpia (*kal*-li-KÔL-pē-ə): the condition of breasts that are beautiful and often larger than ordinary. Derived from Greek *kallos* (beauty) and *kolpos* (breast, womb, vagina).

> *Her male clients were so pleasantly distracted by her **callicolpia** that they found it difficult to look above her neck when speaking with her.*

callicolpos (kal-i-KÔL-pəs): a beautiful bosom. Derived from Greek *kallos* (beauty) and *kolpos* (beast, womb, vagina).

> *The exercise physiologist submitted that men with conventional tastes in women will not find a **callicolpos** on a highly competitive female bodybuilder, since the amount of her body fat will be too low to give pleasing curves to her breasts.*

callicunnate (kal-i-KUN-āt): having beautiful female external genitalia. Derived from Greek *kallos* (beauty) and Latin *cunnus* (the vulva).

*The young man insisted that, if a woman has an unattractive personality, he does not want a relationship with her, regardless of how **callicunnate** she might be.*

callifemoral (kal-li-FEM-ər-əl): having beautiful thighs, a word applied especially to females. Derived from Greek *kallos* (beauty) and Latin *femur* (thigh).

*Since James was especially attracted to feminine legs, and since Sandra was **callifemoral**, he was extremely excited to see her in a bikini.*

callimammapygian (kal-li-mam-ə-PIJ-ē-ən): having beautiful buttocks and breasts. Derived from Greek *kallos* (beauty), Latin *mamma* (breast), and Greek *pyge* (buttocks).

*The playboy said that he is looking for a rich and well-educated woman, preferably sexually adroit and **callimammapygian**.*

callimastian (kal-li-MAS-tē-ən): having beautiful breasts. Derived from Greek *kallos* (beauty) and *mastos* (breast).

*Both Julia Roberts and Sandra Bullock prove that women can be **callimastian** without having unusually large breasts.*

callinymph (*KAL*-li-nimf): a beautiful bride. Derived from Greek *kallos* (beauty) and *nymphe* (bride, nymph).

*When Jennifer Aniston married Brad Pitt, she was doubtless a **callinymph**.*

calliphallic (kal-li-FAL-ik): pertaining to, or having, a beautiful or handsome penis. Derived from Greek *kallos* (beauty) and *phallos* (penis).

*The young woman said that, so long as her future husband has a good heart and a passably attractive face and body, whether he is **calliphallic** won't matter.*

calliphallus (kal-li-FAL-us): a beautiful or handsome penis.

*Chelsea said that even though her boyfriend has a **calliphallus**, it is his personality and character that appeal to her.*

callipygian (kal-li-PIJ-ə-ən): having shapely or beautiful buttocks. Derived from Greek *kallos* (beauty) and *pyge* (buttocks).

*If we are to judge by the popularity of exercise equipment and videotapes for firming up the buttocks, Americans value **callipygian** persons.*

callipygus (kal-LIP-i-gəs): a beautiful female buttocks. Derived from Greek *kallos* (beauty) and *pyge* (buttocks).
A man must exercise care in complimenting a woman he hardly knows on her callipygus.

callisphyrous (kal-li-SFĪ-rus): having beautiful ankles. Derived from Greek *kallos* (beauty) and *sphyron* (ankle).
Had Ayn not been wearing an ankle bracelet, Nathaniel might not have noticed that she was callisphyrous.

callisural (kal-li-SOŎR-əl): having beautiful calves. Derived from Greek *kallos* (beauty) and Latin *sura* (calf of leg).
Because Heather is callisural, her husband, Brian, always insists that she never wear long pants.

callitrema (kal-li-TRĒ-mə): a female with beautiful external genitalia. Derived from Greek *kallos* (beauty) and *trema* (hole).
Rarely will men marry women simply because they are callitremas.

callitrichous (kal-LIT-ri-kəs): having beautiful hair. Derived from Greek *kallos* (beauty) and *thrix* (hair).
Alexander Pope's satirical poem The Rape of the Lock *concerns a woman who prides herself on being callitrichous.*

callomania (kal-ō-MĀN-ē-ə): delusion that one is extraordinarily beautiful. Derived from Greek *kallos* (beauty) and *mania* (madness, craving).
Her callomania made her think that men were attracted to her physical appearance rather than to her unconditional sexual availability.

capnolagnia (kap-nō-LAG-nē-ə): erotic attraction to, and stimulation by, watching others' tobacco smoke. Derived from Greek *kapnos* (smoke) and *lagneia* (lust).
Since smoking is an oral activity that can be performed with varying levels of sexy body language, it is understandable how someone might be affected by capnolagnia.

casimeria (kas-i-MER-ē-e): sexual interest in a brother. Derived from Greek *kasignetos* (brother) and *himeros* (yearning for, desiring).
The sociologist said that casimeria is probably more common than most people think, but it is hidden, since people are usually discouraged from having sex with their siblings.

castrati (ka-STRO-tē): singers castrated when they were boys to preserve the soprano or contralto range of their voices. Derived from Latin *castratus* (castrated male).

> *Some prepubescent male singers of soul music have had pleasant yet feminine-sounding voices, suggestive of the* **castrati***.*

catamenia (*kat-ə-ME̅-ne̅-ə*): a medical term for menstruation. Derived from Greek *katamenios* (monthly).

> *Some men prefer to avoid sex with women during* **catamenia***, and some religions forbid sex with women in that condition.*

catamite (KAT-ə-mīt): a boy kept for homosexual sex, or simply a boy who has homosexual relations with a man. Derived from Latin *catamitus* (from Greek *Ganymedes*, Ganymede, cupbearer of the gods, known for homosexual involvement in relations with some other gods).

> *Oscar Wilde was foolish legally to contest charges that he was a practicing homosexual, because there were some* **catamites** *and male prostitutes who could substantiate those charges.*

cataphilist (ka-TAF-i-list): male submitting to a female. Derived from Greek *kata* (down), *philein* (to love), and -*ist* (one who).

> *Perry loved to be dominated and was quite the* **cataphilist** *in the bedroom.*

catapygon (kat-ə-PI̅-gən): a male homosexual in ancient Greece. Derived from Greek *kata* (down) and *pyge* (buttocks).

> **Catapygons** *and bisexuals in ancient Greece were viewed differently from the way they were viewed in Victorian England.*

catatasis (kə-TAT-ə-sis): a tribal practice of attaching a weight to the head of a penis to lengthen the organ. Derived from Greek *kata* (down) and *tasis* (a stretching).

> *While we do not know whether* **catatasis** *is effective, we do know that most men normally prefer that a certain part of their anatomy not be stretched.*

celerorgasmus (sə-ler-or-GAZ-mus): premature ejaculation, especially in males who achieve orgasm abnormally more quickly than their female partners. Derived from Latin *celer* (swift) and Greek *orgasmos* (swelling).

> *Adam was looking for ways to delay his climaxes because his wife, Eve, found his* **celerogasmus** *frustrating.*

cheilocunnidipity (kī̅-lo̅-kunni-DIP-i-te̅): a mental visualization in which people (especially men) imagine the lips of the woman as the counterpart of the vulva. Supposedly, many ancient prostitutes wore lipstick to suggest the imagery described above, though in modern times the term cheilocunnidipity has been applied to males thought to be overinterested in sex and suffering from **satyriasis** (*see entry*). Derived from Greek *cheilos* (lip), Latin *cunnus* (vulva), and *-dipity* (suffix denoting a condition).

Ryan's intensive gazing at Emily's lips suggested that he was engaged in **cheilocunnidipity.**

cheilophilous (*kī*-LOF-i-ləs): being especially attracted to lips, particularly, female lips. Derived from Greek *cheilos* (lip) and *philein* (to love).

Most women who wear lipstick want to accentuate the beauty of their lips and appeal to **cheilophilous** *men.*

chelonia (ki-LŌN-ē-ə): the practice of releasing sexual excitement by clawing and scratching, observed more often in women than in men. Derived from Greek *chele* (claw).

The scratches on Thurston's back were from Mary Ann's **chelonia.**

chezolagnia (chez-ə-LAG-nē-ə): sexual excitement or gratification from moving one's bowels, often while masturbating. Derived from the Greek *chezo* (to defecate) and *lagneia* (lust).

Known for his **chezolagnia,** *Newt pointed to a box of laxatives and asserted, "There are my aphrodisiacs."*

chimaropia (ki-mə-RŌP-ē-ə): the erotic stare of a person (especially in a man) during love play. Derived from Greek *chimairos* (male goat) and *ops* (eye).

Jan would excite Peter to **chimaropia,** *which in turn would further excite her.*

chirapsis (kī-RAP-sis): the practice of a female's inducing orgasm in a male by the friction of her hand on his phallus. Derived from Greek *cheir* (hand) and *haphe* (a touching).

The prostitute was so deeply concerned about sexually transmissible diseases that she wore special medical gloves when practicing **chirapsis** *on customers.*

chiromania (kī-rə-MĀN-ē-e): masturbation by hand, especially when regarded as excessive. Derived from Greek *cheir* (hand) and *mania* (madness, craving).

Although our law professor said that his hand was sore from lifting weights, we knew that he did not lift weights and suspected **chiromania** *was the cause.*

chordee (KÔR-dē): painful downward curving of the penis, sometimes a side effect of gonorrhea. Derived from French *cordée* (corded).
*When the doctor noticed the man's **chordee**, he tested him for gonorrhea.*

choreophilia (kor-ē-ō-FIL-ē-e): arousal from dancing. Derived from Greek *khoreia* (choral dance) and *philia* (attachment, attraction).
*Sally enjoyed indulging her **choreophilia** on the dance floor.*

chorotripsis (ko-rō-TRIP-sis): the touching or rubbing against one's sex partners while dancing and the consequent sexual excitement, sometimes producing orgasm. Derived from Greek *choros* (dance) and *tripsis* (a rubbing).
*Dancing alone can stir erotic feelings, but experiencing **chorotripsis** from someone to whom one is strongly attracted can be profoundly stimulating.*

chronophilia (*kron*-ə-FIL-ē-ə): attraction to persons who are older or younger than oneself. Derived from Greek *chronos* (time) and *philia* (attachment, attraction).
*In America, **chronophilia** is usually considered more acceptable if it is the man rather than the woman who is the older one in the relationship.*

chymocunnia (*kī*-mə-KUN-ē-ə): the condition in which the vulva is well moistened by lubricating discharges. Derived from Greek *chymos* (juice) and Latin *cunnus* (the vulva).
*Morticia's **chymocunnia** made intercourse not only easier but also more pleasurable for her and Fester.*

cingulomania (*sing*-yə-lō-MĀN-ē-ə): a powerful desire to embrace and hold in one's arms the object of one's attraction, especially a male's desire to hold a female. Derived from Latin *cingulum* (a girdle) and Greek *mania* (madness, craving).
*The prisoner was frustrated, since his wife was separated from him by a thick sheet of glass, preventing him from satisfying his **cingulomania**.*

clinovalent (klī-nō-VĀL-ənt): sexually potent only when lying down. Derived from Greek *klino* (to bend, slope, slant) and Latin *valere* (to be strong).
*While most men may usually prefer to have intercourse while reclining, most men are not **clinovalent**.*

clitorize (KLIT-ur-*īz*): an obsolete verb meaning "to perform female masturbation." Derived from Greek *kleitoris* (clitoris).

*The nun warned her female students that they should use the bathroom to eliminate waste, not to **clitorize**.*

clitoromania (klit-ə-rō-MĀN-ē-ə): sexual desire in a woman viewed by others as "excessive" and "uncontrollable"; nymphomania. Derived from Greek *kleitoris* (clitoris) and *mania* (madness, craving).

The minister said that the pornographic movie Insatiable *should never have been made, because the character played by Marilyn Chambers, especially in the last scene, gives full vent to her **clitoromania**.*

clitoromegaly (klit-ə-rō-MEG-ə-lē): an enlarged clitoris, usually caused by an excess of male sex hormones. Derived from Greek *kleitoris* (clitoris) and *megas* (great).

*After the female bodybuilder spent months taking male hormones, she developed **clitoromegaly**.*

clunicentric (*klōō*-ni/ne-SEN-trik): tending to focus or center one's attention on the buttocks, a word applied especially to males. Derived from Latin *clunis* (buttocks) and Greek *kentron* (center of a circle).

On the classic TV show Dick Van Dyke, *Mary Tyler Moore, who played Laura Petrie, was cautioned against wearing tight-fitting chinos, lest she should offend people's sensibilities or unduly appeal to **clunicentric** men.*

Clytemnestra complex: a love triangle in which a woman falls in love with a male relative of her husband, and kills her spouse to be with that relative. Derived from the Greek myth in which Clytemnestra falls in love with her husband's cousin, and kills her husband to be with her lover.

*Mary fell in love with her husband's brother Jack and killed her husband, exemplifying the **Clytemnestra complex**.*

cnemopalmia (*nē*-mə-POL-mē-ə): male preference for a woman's legs, as in a "leg man." Derived from Greek *kneme* (leg) and Latin *palma* (prize).

*Pete was so absorbed in **cnemopalmia** that he would rarely notice anything about a woman that was higher than her thighs.*

cnemotaxis (*nē*-mə-TAKS-əs): the stimulating and attracting effect a woman's legs have upon a man. Derived from Greek *kneme* (leg) and *taxis* (arrangement).

*Many men like miniskirts because of **cnemotaxis**.*

coital ectrimma (KŌ-ĭ-təl EK-trim-ə): a sore place on the male or female sex organ produced by friction during intercourse. Derived from Latin *coitus* (sexual intercourse) and Greek *ektrimma* (an ulcer produced by friction).

*Harry copulated with such energy that he formed a **coital ectrimma** on his organ.*

coital mancinism (KŌ-ĭ-təl MAN-tsə-*nizəm*): (male) awkwardness in performing sexual intercourse. Derived from Latin *coitus* (sexual intercourse) and Italian *mancino* (left-handed).

*People should be excused for displaying **coital mancinism** when having intercourse for the first time.*

coitant (KŌ-i-tənt): the male in male-female intercourse. Derived from Latin *coitus* (sexual intercourse).

*Most heterosexual males, when viewing pornography, do not care whether the **coitant** is attractive, since their eyes are drawn more to the women.*

coitante (kō-i-TÄNT): the female in male-female intercourse. Derived from Latin *coitus* (sexual intercourse).

*In her pictorial book Sex, Madonna was quite the versatile **coitante**, equally at home with not only different men but also different species.*

coitobalnism (*kō*-i-tō-BAL-niz-əm): practice of having sexual intercourse in a filled bathtub. Derived from Latin *coitus* (sexual intercourse) and *balneum* (bath).

*The young bachelor wanted to "christen" his new bathtub by experiencing **coitobalnism** with his girlfriend.*

coitocentric (*kō*-i-tō-SEN-trik): center one's erotic energies on sexual intercourse rather than on foreplay. Derived from Latin *coitus* (sexual intercourse) and Greek *kentron* (center of a circle).

*The sex therapist asserted that most women do not fully enjoy sex with **coitocentric** men because women generally prefer romantic foreplay before intercourse.*

coitolimia (*kō*-i-tə-LIM/LĒM-ē-e): hunger for sexual intercourse. Derived from Latin *coitus* (sexual intercourse) and Greek *limos* (hunger).

*Brock's **coitolimia** was so great that he had intercourse with his girlfriend while standing in a pool and surrounded by strangers.*

coitoperissia (*kō*-i-tə-pe-RIZ-ē-e): excessive indulgence in sexual intercourse. Derived from Latin *coitus* (sexual intercourse) and Greek *perisseia* (abundance, surplus); related to *perissos* (extraordinary).

While people will sometimes disagree over when indulgence in sexual intercourse is excessive, most people believe that any man who has had sex with more than twenty thousand women can reasonably be accused of **coitoperissia.**

coitophthoria (*kō*-i-tə-FTHOR-ē-ə): the loss of interest in ordinary sexual practices and the accompanying desire for unusual sexual practices. Derived from Latin *coitus* (sexual intercourse) and Greek *phthora* (destruction, corruption).

Some people believe the former President Clinton's use of a cigar as a sex aid reflects **coitophthoria.**

coitus acceptus (KŌ-i-təs äk-SEP-tus): Latin for sexual intercourse welcome by the female participant.

The politician insisted that, although he was unfaithful to his wife countless times, every sexual act he performed was **coitus acceptus.**

coitus adulterinus (KŌ-i-təs a-dul-te-RĒN-us): out-of-wedlock sexual intercourse that begets a child, or simply sexual intercourse involving adultery.

The prominent evangelist and political leader was embarrassed by the revelation of his **coitus adulterinus,** *which produced a child he has agreed to support.*

coitus Bacchicus (KŌ-i-təs BÄK-i-kus): Latin for sexual intercourse that is part of an orgy. Derived from the name of the Roman god of wine, fertility, vegetation, and the dramatic arts.

The steamy movie Eyes Wide Shut *depicted persons who were used to seeing unrestrained orgies in which acts of* **coitus Bacchicus** *were an integral part.*

coitus delicatus (KŌ-i-təs del-i-KÄ-tus): Latin for any form of contraceptive sexual intercourse engaged in only for pleasure.

The priest told the married couple that their marriage did not entitle them to **coitus delicatus,** *viewed by the church as a misuse of their sexual organs.*

coitus fecundus (KŌ-i-təs fi-KOŎN-dus): Latin for sexual intercourse producing pregnancy. Derived from *coitus* (sexual intercourse) and *fecundus* (fruitful).

The man told us that in his town nonmarital **coitus delicatus** [see entry] *was subject to less disapproval than nonmarital* **coitus fecundus.**

coitus interruptus (KŌ-i-təs in-tə-RUP'təs): Latin for interrupted sexual intercourse in which the male withdraws just before ejaculation.

Some men intend to engage in **coitus interruptus** *as a method of birth control, but discover, often too late, that it is risky.*

colobosis (käl-lə-BŌ-sis): the amputation of the male sex organ in a jealous rage. Derived from Greek *kolobos* (docked, curtailed) and *-osis* (suffix designating a state or condition). (*See* **peotomy.**)

Men who give their spouses a reason to be jealous and who consequently suffer **colobosis** *know the meaning of the cliché that there is no wrath like the wrath of a woman scorned.*

colpalgia (*käl*-PAL-j(ē)ə): feeling of discomfort or pain in the vagina from childbirth, frequent intercourse, or masturbation. Derived from Greek *kolpos* (womb, breast, vagina) and *algos* (pain).

Monica's boyfriend apologized for the **colpalgia** *caused by his unusually placed cigar.*

colpectasia (*käl*-pek-TĀZHĀ): distention or dilation of the vaginal canal, as from childbirth, frequent intercourse, or masturbation. Derived from Greek *kolpos* (womb, breast, vagina) and *ektasis* (distention).

Rose's **colpectasia** *was due to her having produced nine children.*

colpismus (*käl*-PIZ-mus): a spastic contraction of the vagina, as from fear of sexual intercourse. Derived from Greek *kolpos* (womb, breast, vagina) and *-ismos* (stuff, suffix denoting a state, condition, or doctrine).

Because of Pamela's fear of sexual intercourse, she experienced a **colpismus** *on her wedding night.*

colpophronate (*käl*-pe-FRŌ-nāt): to think excessively about female external genitalia. Derived from Greek *kolpos* (womb, breast, vagina) and *phren* (mind).

"Some men think obsessively about breasts, but I **colpophronate,***" said the grandiloquent English professor.*

colpoxerosis (käl-pok-se-RŌ-sis): abnormal dryness of the interior of the vagina. Derived from Greek *kolpos* (womb, breast, vagina), *xeros* (dry), and *-osis* (suffix designating a condition or state).

Marta found intercourse less pleasant than usual because of her **colpoxerosis.**

concupiscencia (kon-kū-pi-SEN(T)-shē-ə): Latin for "ardent desire," "lust."

The belief that all *sex is an expression of sin, lust, or* **concupiscencia** *was embraced by St. Augustine.*

condonation (*kondō*-NĀ-shən): a legal concept in which an illegal act, such as adultery, is not prosecuted or used as a grounds for a lawsuit because the aggrieved party forgives the offending party. A spouse who resumes sexual relations with an adulterous partner, according to the law, condones and forgives the partner's behavior. Derived from Latin *condonare* (to give, remit, forgive).

After Jerry committed adultery, he arranged to sleep with his wife as soon as possible for **condonation**.

contrariation (kon-trārē-Ā-shən): sexual pleasure by males from tantalizing or teasing females, as by displaying their naked bodies without allowing the females to touch them; also the tantalizing action involved. Derived from Latin *contrarius* (opposed, contrary to) and *-tion* (suffix designating an act, state, or condition).

Women often resent men who engage in **contrariation** *because most people do not enjoy someone's deliberately frustrating them.*

contrectation (kon-trek-TĀ-shun): fondling or foreplay. Derived from Latin *contrectare* (to touch, feel).

The nun insisted that, when she is the chaperone at the dance, there will be absolutely no **contrectation**.

Coolidge effect: the tendency of males who are no longer capable of being aroused by the same female to be energetic and eager at a moment's notice in the presence of a new partner. According to an anecdote, the origin of the phrase Coolidge effect stems from an incident involving President and Mrs. Coolidge. During a tour of a chicken farm, Mrs. Coolidge asked a farmer how often a cock can mount a hen. The farmer replied "about [say] forty times a day," whereupon Mrs. Coolidge replied, "Please tell this to my husband." After the farmer conveyed that information to President Coolidge, Coolidge asked whether the cock mounted the same hen forty times and was informed that the cock mounted forty *different* hens. Upon learning that piece of information, President Coolidge replied, "Please tell *this* to my wife."

Over the years Hillary Rodham Clinton has seen the **Coolidge effect** *operate with almost metronomic regularity.*

cool sex values: a system of sexual values based on flexible sex roles and types of relationships, an open sensuality, egalitarian relations, and the ab-

sence of sexual stereotypes. The expression is used in contradistinction to
hot sex values (*see entry*).

> *Anyone who wants to know how **cool sex values** differ from **hot sex***
> ***values** should think about how the sexual beliefs and attitudes of*
> Playboy's *Hugh Hefner differ from those of evangelist Jerry Falwell.*

coprography (ko-PROG-rə-fē): (i) the impulse to write or draw obscene
material, especially words relating to excrement or anal sex; (ii) the material, such as graffiti, produced from the impulse. Derived from Greek *kopros*
(dung) and *-graphos* (writing).

> *Our parochial school teacher assured us that, when the Bible says that*
> *God will spread dung on the face of disobedient priests* [Malachi 2:1–3],
> *it is condemning unrighteousness, not promoting **coprography**.*

coprolagnia (kop-rə-LAG-nē-ə): derivation of sexual pleasure from
watching, smelling, handling, or having other contact with human excrement, especially that which has come from a member of the opposite sex.
Derived from Greek *kopros* (dung) and *lagneia* (lust).

> *We did not learn about Jethro's **coprolagnia** until we saw jars of Jane's*
> *feces in his closet.*

coprolalia (kop-rə-LĀL-ē-ə): the impulse, supposedly irresistible, to utter
obscenities, especially slang words concerning excrement. Derived from
Greek *kopros* (dung) and *lalia* (talk, chatter, prattle).

> *While "involuntary **coprolalia**" is considered a symptom of Tourette's*
> *disorder, many persons choose to utter obscenities, especially during sex, to*
> *arouse themselves or their partners.*

coprophagy (ko-PROF ə jē): the eating of feces, especially for sexual
arousal. Derived from Greek *kopros* (dung) and *phagein* (to eat).

> *While **coprophagy** does not appeal to most people, people have engaged*
> *in it for centuries. In fact, an ancient aphrodisiac contained semen mixed*
> *with hawk feces.*

coprophemia (kop-rə-FĒM-ē-ə): a psychiatric disorder in which obscene
speech is an essential prelude or accompaniment to sexual arousal. Derived
from Greek *kopros* (dung) and *-phemia* (speech).

> *Since Pat could not break Dick from his **coprophemia**, she learned to*
> *tolerate his obscenities during their sex.*

coprophilia (kop-rə-FIL-ē-e): marked sexual interest in excrement. Such
interest can include constant jokes about excrement, sexual excitement dur-

ing defecation, and the hoarding of feces. Derived from the Greek *kopros* (dung) and *philia* (attachment, attraction).

When his wife called him a "brown noser," we had no idea that she was alluding to his coprophilia.

coproscopist (kop-*rō*-SKŌ-pist): someone who derives sexual pleasure from watching people defecate. Derived from Greek *kopros* (feces), *skopein* (to view), and *-ist* (suffix meaning "one who").

We did not learn that Manny was a coproscopist until we happened to catch him drilling a hole into a wall in the girls' restroom.

copula carnalis (KOP-yə-lə kar-NÄ-lis): a legal term derived from Latin for intercourse between husband and wife. Derived from Latin *copula* (bond, tie, connection) and *carnis* (flesh).

It is difficult to find sexual activity legal in the commonwealth of Virginia except copula carnalis, performed, of course, in the missionary position.

copula fornicatoria (KOP-yə-lə for-nik-TOR-ē-ə): a legal term for intercourse between a man and a prostitute. Derived from Latin *copula* (bond, tie, connection) and *fornix* (vault, brothel). "Fornix" is, by the way, a name for the archlike vault or upper space of the vaginal canal, derived from the name of the space under the arches of Roman viaducts where prostitutes would work.

Actor Hugh Grant's copula fornicatoria might have helped his acting career.

coquette (kō-KET): a woman who intentionally attracts men without having any desire to consummate any sexual relationship with them. In colloquial English, a coquette might be called a "flirt," and in vulgar slang she might be called a "cockteaser." Although the term is from French *coquet* (flirtatious man), it appeared in English in the early 1600s.

Men who hunger for sex can become deeply frustrated by coquettes.

corikanthosis (*kori*-kan-THŌ-sis): development of female characteristics in a young girl. Derived from Greek *korikos* (girlish) and *anthos* (bloom).

Michelle's corikanthosis and her initial interest in boys occurred simultaneously.

crurocentric (krōōr-ə-SEN-trik, krōō-rō/rə-SEN-trik): centering one's erotic attention on legs. Derived from Latin *crus* (leg) and Greek *kentron* (center of a circle).

*Murray was so **crurocentric** that he rarely even noticed any woman's body above the thighs.*

crurophilous (kroo-ROF-i-ləs): especially attracted to legs. Derived from Latin *crus* (leg) and *philein* (to love).
*"Leg men" are, by definition, **crurophilous**.*

cryptoscopophilia (krip-tō-skō-pō-FIL-ē-ə): attraction to looking through windows as a Peeping Tom. Derived from Greek *kryptos* (hidden), *skopein* (to observe), and *philia* (attachment, attraction).
*Because of her neighbor's **cryptoscopophilia**, Mary felt impelled to buy thicker draperies.*

cryptovestiphilia (krip-tō-vesti-FIL-ē-ə): attraction to women's undergarments. Derived from Greek *kryptos* (hidden), Latin *vestis* (garments), and Greek *philia* (attachment, attraction).
*His vast collection of "Victoria's Secret" catalogs, bras, panties, and garters led us to believe that Martin was involved in transvestism or **cryptovestiphilia**.*

cunniknismos (kən-i-NISMUS): the practice of tickling the vulva, as with the fingers or tongue. Derived from Latin *cunnus* (vulva) and Greek *knizo* (to tickle, tease).
*Martha told George that, because she was ticklish and on her first date, **cunniknismos** was out of the question.*

cunnilalia (*kən*-ni-LĀL-ē-ə): conversation—especially when obscene—about female genitals. Derived from the Latin *cunnus* (vulva) and the Greek *lalia* (talk, chatter).
The radio shock jock Howard Stern has made millions of dollars because of his talk about breasts and his ability to engage in cunnilalia.

cunnilingant (*kən*-ni-LING-ənt): the female on whom oral-genital sex or **cunnilingus** (*see entry*) is performed. Derived from Latin *cunnus* (vulva) and *lingere* (to lick).
*Our professor speculated that more women prefer being **cunnilingants** to performing oral sex on men.*

cunnilinguist (kənə-LINGWIST): a person who performs oral sex on the vulva. Derived from Latin *cunnus* (vulva) and *lingere* (lick).
*When a hearing-impaired student heard the eminent scholar Noam Chomsky's being introduced as a "cunning linguist," he asked Chomsky why a **cunnilinguist** would want everyone to know his sexual habits.*

cunnilingus (kənə-LING-əs): oral stimulation of the clitoris or vulva. Derived from Latin *cunnus* (vulva) and *lingere* (lick).

A man who learns a marketable trade and the art of **cunnilingus** *will never go hungry.*

cunniphilemia (kə-nə-fi-LĒM-e-ə): the kissing of the female genitalia. Derived from Latin *cunnus* (vulva) and Greek *philema* (a kiss).

When Jerry caught George performing **cunniphilemia** *on Elaine, George, embarrassed, responded that he was looking for ticks.*

cunnitripsis (kə-nə-TRIP-sis): the rubbing of the female genitals by a man. Derived from Latin *cunnus* (the external female organ) and Greek *tripsis* (a rubbing).

The former president was not charged with **cunnitripsis** *and other sexual acts, but with lying about such acts under oath.*

cunnorasia (kən-ə-RĀZHə): the habit of rubbing or scratching the vulva by manipulating the skirt or dress over the sexual organs, usually to alleviate itching. Derived from Latin *cunnus* (vulva) and *rado* (to scratch).

The girl's **cunnorasia** *was not a form of masturbation but a response to an itch.*

cyesolagnia (sī-ēs-ə-LAG-nē-ə): sexual arousal from pregnant women. Derived from Greek *kyesis* (pregnancy) and *lagneia* (lust).

Because of the orderly's **cyesolagnia**, *he was forbidden to work in the maternity ward.*

cyprinophobia (si-pri-nə-FŌB-ē-ə): excessive fear of lewd women or prostitutes, including their manners and language. Derived from Greek *Kypros* (Cyprus, the legendary birthplace of Aphrodite, goddess of love) and *phobos* (fear).

We knew that the conservative talk show host's **cyprinophobia** *would prevent her from enjoying the Madonna concert.*

cypripareunia (sip-ri-pə-ROŎ-nē-ə): sex with a prostitute. Derived from Greek *Kypros* (Cyprus, the legendary birthplace of Aphrodite, goddess of love) and *pareunos* (lying beside, bedfellow).

The actor's **cypripareunia** *did not hurt his career.*

D

dacrylagnia (dak-ri-LAG-nē-ə): attraction to, or stimulation by, a woman's tears. Derived from Greek *dakryon* (tear) and *lagneia* (lust).
*We wondered whether Jason's **dacrylagnia** would be excited when Michelle peeled the onions.*

dactylate (DAK-ti-*lat*): to introduce a finger into the vagina, especially for masturbation. Derived from Greek *daktylos* (finger).
*Rebecca's father told her date that the last time someone **dactylated** his daughter, he ended up in the hospital with some broken fingers.*

dasofallation (das-ō-fal-LĀ-shən): sexual intercourse in a forest or wooded area. Derived from Greek *dasos* (thicket, forest), *phallos* (penis), and *-tion* (act or state of).
*The forest ranger told us that in some remote areas of national parks men and women will sometimes engage in **dasofallation**.*

dasyproctic (*das*-i-PROK-tik): hairy-assed, often used to describe certain monkeys. Derived from Greek *dasys* (thick with hair) and *proktos* (rectum).
*Because Christopher did not enjoy being **dasyproctic**, he would regularly shave his buttocks.*

decoromedia (dek-ə-rō-MĒD-ē-ə): the summation of what is considered the correct sexual procedure for the penis before and during intercourse. Derived from Latin *deceo* (to be suitable or correct) and Greek *medos* (the male organ).
*The sexually awkward young man thought that he might never master the skills necessary for **decoromedia**.*

delibidinalization (dē-li-bid-i-nəl-ī-ZĀ-shən): the reduction, elimination, or sublimation of one's sex drive. Derived from Latin *de-* (from, away), *libido* (lust), and *-ization* (suffix indicating a process).
*Before Johnny used to focus all his energy on sex; now he is consumed by an interest in playing sports, reflecting a **delibidinalization**.*

Delilah syndrome: a pattern of female "promiscuity" in which women desire to control their partners and render them helpless. Derived from the biblical figure of Delilah, who exploited and controlled men, much as her father had exploited and controlled her in her earlier life.
*Janice, who had sexual relations with numerous men, would use sex to dominate them in ways suggestive of the **Delilah syndrome**.*

delinolagnia (del-in-ō-LAG-nē-ə): lustfulness in the afternoon. Derived from Greek *delinos* (in the afternoon) and *lagneia* (lust).
> *Ryan's* **delinolagnia** *caused him to look for some "afternoon delight."*

demi-vierge (dem-ē-vē-URZH): an old-fashioned term for a girl who is technically a virgin but who engages in many sexual activities short of intercourse; also known as a "technical virgin." Derived from French for "half-virgin."
> *A* **demi-vierge,** *Buffy had enjoyed every form of sexual contact except sexual intercourse, which she thought should be reserved for marriage.*

dendrophilia (den-drō-FIL-ē-ə): sexual interest in trees. Derived from Greek *dendron* (tree) and *philia* (attachment, attraction).
> *When we heard that Mr. Sylvan was a "tree-hugger," we thought that he was involved in environmentalism, not* **dendrophilia***.*

deonteur (dē-on-TUR): a man learned in the art of making love. Derived from Greek *deon* (what is binding or necessary).
> *Wednesday defended her infidelity by asserting that her affair with a* **deonteur** *might spark her marriage.*

derrierroscopia (der-ē-errō-SKŌP-ē-ə): preoccupation with watching a person's buttocks or derriere. Derived from French for "behind" (buttocks) and Greek *skopein* (to observe).
> *John's* **derrierroscopia** *would sometimes prompt him intentionally to leave last to have a good view of those in line before him.*

detumescence (dē-tōō-MES-əns): the loss of an erection, especially after an orgasm. Derived from Latin *de* (down) and *tumere* (to swell).
> *During* **detumescence***, the male organ is usually particularly sensitive.*

deuterition (dōō-ter-ISH-ən): a second act of intercourse, shortly after the first. Derived from Greek *deuteros* (second) and Latin *coition* (sexual intercourse).
> *Although Kenny enjoyed* **deuterition***, he told his wife that he was too tired for a second bout.*

Diana complex: a psychiatric expression for a woman's deep-seated wish to be a man. Derived probably from the Roman goddess Diana, who played a masculine role as goddess of hunting and protector of women.
> *I told my friend that a woman could have some masculine-appearing attributes without having the* **Diana complex***.*

diaphanophilia (dī-a-fan-ō-FIL-ē-ə): attraction to viewing nudity through sheer fabrics. Derived from Greek *diaphainein* (to show through or to be transparent) and *philia* (attachment, attraction).

*Occasionally, artsy pornographic movies will appeal to **diaphanophilia** by photographing sex through sheer fabrics.*

diapiresalgia (dī-ə-pir-e-SAL-jē-ə): pain felt by a male when pushing a large organ through a small vagina, as in that of a virgin. Derived from Greek *dia* (through), *piresis* (a pushing), and *algos* (pain).

*Roger thought that if he had used a lubricant when having relations with his small wife, he might have avoided **diapiresalgia**.*

diapnolagnia (dī-ap-nō-LAG-nē-ə): sexual stimulation from someone's blowing in one's ear. Derived from Greek *diapnein* (to breathe through) and *lagneia* (lust).

*Cornelia's ecstasy from George's blowing in her ear could mean only one thing: she must have **diapnolagnia**.*

diasteunia (dī-as-TŌO-nē-ə): the practice of sleeping in separate beds, as by husband and wife, to avoid sexual temptation. Derived from Greek *diastatos* (separated) and *eune* (bed).

*Many modern persons can't understand **diasteunia** because they think that husbands and wives should sleep in bed together to facilitate sexual experiences.*

dippoldism (dip-POL-dizəm): sexual arousal from abusing children, especially by flogging them. Derived from the name of a sadistic German tutor, Andreas Dippold, who, in the early twentieth century, was convicted of manslaughter after the death of one of his students.

*The manager of the day care business assured the parent that **dippoldism** is absolutely forbidden by anyone in her employ.*

dishabilloerigesis (dis-ə-bēl-ō-eri-JĒ-sis): the act of provoking sexual interest by deliberate undressing. Derived from French *deshabiller* (to undress) and Greek *erigesis* (excitation).

*Because of the human capacity to gain enjoyment from visual images associated with sex and anticipated pleasure, **dishabilloerigesis** can have a potent effect on people.*

diurnovalent (dī-ur-nō-VĀL-ənt): potent mainly or only during the day, an unusual condition except for persons suffering from physical or psychological problems that occur especially at night. Derived from Latin *dies* (day) and *valero* (to be strong).

*A neurotic person frightened by the night, Woody was **diurnovalent**.*

divine monosyllable: a nineteenth-century euphemism for "cunt," an obscene expression for "vagina."

*Calling a woman the obscene slang four-letter equivalent of the **divine monosyllable** is usually rude and sexist, attempting to reduce her to a mere sex object.*

docking: a form of masturbation involving two uncircumcised men. The foreskin of one partner is pulled back, and the other man's foreskin is stretched over the tip of his penis. The two penises are then stroked so that the skin is moved back and forth over the two glans.

*Before we knew that the two men were gay and were not on a boat, we thought that **docking** was only a nautical maneuver.*

dolichophallic (dol-i-kō-FAL-ik): having a long penis. Derived from the Greek *dolichos* (long) and *phallos* (penis).

*We could not believe that the Clarence Thomas hearings descended to discussion of **dolichophallic** porn stars.*

Dorian love: an obsolete term for "male homosexuality." Derived from the alleged practices of the Dorian tribe, whose members conquered the Peloponnesians of southern Greece in the twelfth century B.C.E.

The ancient Greeks believed that participating in Dorian love and discharging the responsibilities in military life were quite harmonious.

dulcicunnia (dul-si-KUN-ē-ə): the condition of having a sweet-smelling vulva or vagina. Derived from Latin *dulcis* (sweet) and *cunnus* (vulva).

*The executive was chided for publicly complimenting his secretary on her **dulcicunnia**.*

dulcistomia (dul-si-STŌM-ē-ə): the condition of having a mouth sweet enough to kiss. Derived from Latin *dulcis* (sweet) and Greek *stoma* (mouth).

*Allison's **dulcistomia** made kissing her at least as pleasurable as having intercourse with her.*

dyscalligynia (dis-cal-li-JIN-ē-ə): antipathy for beautiful women, as from male frustration due to rejection. Derived from Greek *dys-* (difficult), *kallos* (beauty), and *gune, gyn-* (woman).

*Otis was rejected by so many beautiful women that his **dyscalligynia** was almost inevitable.*

dysmorphophilia (dis-mor-fō-FIL-ē-ə): attraction to, or arousal from, physical deformities in one's sexual partner. Derived from Greek *dys-* (bad), *morphe* (form), and *philia* (attachment, attraction). Persons affected by dysmorphophilia may feel especially attracted to persons with scars, mastectomies, club feet, and other unusual features. Such persons may also be attracted to dwarfs, hunchbacks, or those with various handicaps. The attraction may stem from compassion, a desire for novelty, or a desire to feel in control of a partner unlikely to leave for someone else.

*It is at least possible that some of the many sexual partners of the poet Lord Byron had **dysmorphophilia** and were attracted to him partly because of his club foot.*

dysorgasmia (dis-or-GAZ-mē-ə): a male orgasm achieved only after prolonged effort, possibly including erotic visualization and other strategies. Derived from Greek *dys-* (bad, difficult), *orgasmos* (swelling), and *-ia* (suffix designating a condition).

*Robert's **dysorgasmia** so enervated him that he gave up sex for two years.*

dyspareunia (dis-pa-ROO-nē-ə): a medical term for intercourse that is difficult or painful for the woman. Derived from Greek *dys-* (difficult) and *pareunos* (lying beside, bedfellow).

So egocentric was Hugh that he was completely indifferent to his wife's ***dyspareunia***.

E

ecdemolagnia (ek-dem-ō-LAG-nē-ə): the tendency to be more lustful away from home. Derived from the Greek *ekdemos* (away from home) and *lagneia* (lust).

*The psychiatrist expressed concern over his son's **ecdemolagnia** during the first year of college.*

ecdyosis (ek-dī-Ō-sis): exhibitionism in which persons derive sexual pleasure from disrobing in front of others. Derived from Greek *ekdyein* (to take off, strip off) and *-osis* (suffix designating a condition).

*Mardi Gras celebrations are ideal for women who practice **ecdyosis**.*

ecdysiasm (ek-DIZĒ-azəm): an urge to remove one's clothes, especially to stimulate others; striptease. Derived from Greek *ekdyein* (to take off, to strip off).

*Michelle gave up teaching to take up **ecdysiasm** because she could make a great deal more money revealing her body than imparting the contents of her mind.*

ecdysiast (ek-DIZĒ-*ast*): a stripper. Derived from *ekdyein* (to take off, to strip off).
*In 9½ Weeks, Kim Basinger acted as an **ecdysiast** just for Mickey Rourke in a memorable scene.*

edeomania (ed-ē-ō-MĀN-ē-ə): arousal from, and obsession with, genitalia. Derived from Greek *aidoion* (private parts, genitals) and *mania* (madness, craving).
*Marvin was so overtaken by his **edeomania** that he filled his walls with dozens of pictures of genitalia.*

ego-dystonic homosexuality (Ē-gō dis-TON-ik *hō*-mə-*sek*-shōo-AL-i-tē): homosexuality that is experienced as distressing, distasteful, and shameful by its possessor. Many psychiatrists have defined the rejection of one's homosexuality and its attendant conflict as a distinct disorder. Derived from Latin *ego* (self), Greek *dys-* (bad), and Greek *tonos* (sound, pitch).
*Psychiatrist Dr. Thomas Szasz questions the concept of **ego-dystonic homosexuality** because he thinks it is insulting and arbitrary to define a homosexual person's difficulty with self-acceptance as a distinct disorder when we would rightly reject describing a Black American who has difficulty with his or her identity as an ego-dystonic African American.*

ego-syntonic homosexuality (Ē-gō sin-TON-ik *ho*-mə-*sek*-shōo-AL-i-tē): homosexuality that is considered acceptable and self-consistent by its possessor. Derived from Latin *ego* (self), Greek *syn-* (same), and Greek *tonos* (sound, pitch).
*Many psychiatrists do not regard **ego-syntonic homosexuality** as a disorder, since it need not impair social and emotional functioning.*

ejaculatio deficiens (i-jak-yə-LĀ-shē-ō de-FIS-e-əns): Latin for a failure to ejaculate during intercourse.
*His **ejaculatio deficiens**, due to a medical condition, made John less concerned about using methods of birth control than he would have been otherwise.*

ejaculatio praecox (i-jak-yə-LĀ-shē-ō PRĒ-koks): a medical term derived from Latin for premature ejaculation.
*Since sexual stamina is usually a requirement for male porn stars, a man with **ejaculatio praecox** would probably not last as an actor in the porn business.*

ejaculatio retardata (i-jak-yə-LĀ-shē-ō rē-tar-DÄ-ta): a medical term from Latin for excessively delayed ejaculation during intercourse, possibly because of anxiety, insecurity, or aging.

*Because of Benny's low level of physical fitness and **ejaculatio retardata**, he would become exhausted before he was able to climax.*

Electra complex: in psychoanalytic theory, the sexual attraction felt by a girl for her father, usually accompanied by a sense of competition with, and hostility to, the girl's mother. In the Greek myth, Clytemnestra and her lover, Aegisthus, murder Clytemnestra's husband, Agamemnon, so that they can marry. Then Electra, Clytemnestra's daughter, persuaded her brother Orestes to kill their mother. In current psychoanalytic usage, the expression **Oedipus complex** (*see entry*) has displaced Electra complex to apply to the attachment of both sons and daughters to their cross-sex parent.

*According to psychoanalytic theory, a female with an **Electra complex** blames her mother for depriving her of a penis.*

eleutherophilist (ə-lōō-thə-ROF-i-list): a person who believes in free love. Derived from Greek *eleutheria* (freedom) and *philein* (to love).

*Anyone whose motto is "sex, drugs, and rock 'n' roll" is an **eleutherophilist**.*

ellipseur (ə-lip-SUR): a man who omits all foreplay and goes straight to sexual intercourse with haste. Derived from Greek *elleipo* (to leave out or undone).

*The prostitute said that her customer was so unattractive that she was happy that he was an **ellipseur**.*

emetophilia (i-met-ə-FIL-e-ə): arousal from vomit; also known as a "Roman shower." Derived from Greek *emein* (to vomit) and *philia* (attachment, attraction).

*Persons affected by **emetophilia** will sometimes drink wine or urine, and then vomit it out, sometimes onto partners.*

endogamy (en-DOG-ə-mē): the custom of marrying within one's tribe, family, clan, religion, or other social unit. Derived from Greek *endo* (within) and *gamos* (marriage).

*Modern Jews do not practice **endogamy** to the degree that Jews did several generations ago.*

endytolagnia (en-dē-tō-LAG-nē-ə): sexual preference for persons who are fully clothed rather than naked. Derived from Greek *endytos* (clothed) and *lagneia* (lust).

*Danny's **endytolagnia** led him to insist that the prostitute leave on nearly all her clothes.*

endytophallist (en-dē-TOF-ə-list): a male who prefers to have sex with women who are dressed. Derived from the Greek *endytos* (clothed) and *phallos* (penis).
*The **endytophallist** told the young woman in the bikini that she had not nearly enough on to entice him to have sex.*

English vice: a slang term for flagellation (whipping), traditionally a popular practice in English brothels; also known as "English culture."
*The well-traveled aristocrat, who enjoyed being on the receiving end of the **English vice**, asserted that some of the best whips are in English riding shops.*

enspasmation (en-spaz-MĀ-shən): the embracing of a woman against her will. Derived from Greek *en* (in), *aspazomai* (embrace).
*Since women have a right to say "no," even to embraces, men should avoid **enspasmation**.*

entomophilia (en-tə-mō-FIL-ē-ə): arousal from insects or the use of insects in sex. Derived from Greek *entomon* (insert) and *philia* (attachment, attraction).
*When Mary rubbed her genital hair with honey, and pulled out a small jar of ants, John had a strong suspicion that she was affected by **entomophilia**.*

entorexia (en-tə-REKS-ē-ə): the ability to repress one's sexual cravings. Derived from Greek *entos* (within) and Latin/Greek *orexis* (desire).
*We complimented the nuns on their self-control and especially their **entorexia**.*

eonism (Ē-ə-nizəm): transvestism. Derived from the name of nineteenth-century French political adventurer Charles Eon de Beaumont, who for many years posed as a woman.
*Persons practicing **eonism** take pleasure in cross-dressing.*

eopareunia (ēə-pə-ROͅO-nē-ə): sex by young people. Derived from Greek *eos* (dawn) and *pareunos* (lying beside, bedfellow).
*The conservative talk show host asserted that we must emphasize abstinence rather than safe sex if we are to reduce **eopareunia**.*

eopothesis (ēə-po-THĒSIS): early development of the sex drive. Derived from Greek *eos* (dawn) and *potheo* (to long for, yearn after).

*A child experiencing **eopothesis** might think that, because he has sexual
desires, he ought to be allowed to satisfy them in the ways that adults might.*

eopothozemia (ēə-po-thə-ZĒM-ē-ə): early loss of sexual desire. Derived
from Greek *eos* (dawn), *potheo* (to long for, yearn after), and *zemia* (loss).
   *At twenty-five, Jeremy experienced **eopothozemia**, leading him to see no
   point in dating.*

ephebophilia (ə-fēb-ə-FIL-ē-ə): a man's attraction to a boy who has recently reached puberty, common in ancient Greece. Derived from Greek
epi- (on, upon, to), *hebe* (youth, youthful prime), and *philia* (attachment,
attraction).
   *Known for, among other things, his **ephebophilia**, the Roman emperor
   Tiberius would call his boys "minnows."*

epicene (EPə-sēn): (i) having characteristics typical of the opposite sex; (ii)
lacking the typical characteristics of either sex; (iii) having characteristics of
both sexes; androgynous; (iv) lacking vigor. Derived from Greek *epi-* (on,
upon, to) and *koinos* (common).
   *The **epicene** girl was always wanting to play football and climb trees.*

eproctolagniac (i-prok-tō-LAG-nē-ak): person aroused from others' flatulence. Derived from Latin *e-* (out, out of), Greek *proktos* (rectum), and
Greek *lagneia* (lust).
   *We first came to suspect that Buford was an **eproctolagniac** after we saw
   him laughing as he was buying two dozen cans of baked beans for his
   wife.*

eproctophile (i-PROK-tō-*fīl*): a person who sexually enjoys farting.
Derived from Latin *e-* (out, out of), Greek *proktos* (rectum), and Greek
philein (to love).
   *Few experiences are as unpleasant as being trapped in an elevator with an
   eproctophile who has just eaten beans.*

eproctophilia (i-*prok*-tō-FIL-ē-ə): arousal from flatulence. Derived from
Greek *proktos* (rectum) and *philia* (attachment, attraction).
   *Because of Allison's **eproctophilia**, Brad would sometimes expel gas in
   bed, and then pull the covers over both of them.*

equisexuality (ek-wi-*sek*-shōō-AL-i-tē): an old term for "homosexuality."
Derived from Latin *aequalis* (like, same) and *sexus* (sex).
   *More than a few people have wondered whether the actor James Dean
   preferred heterosexuality, bisexuality, or **equisexuality**.*

erastophiliac (i-*ras*-tō-FIL-ē-ak): a person having a strong desire to delve in, and gossip about, the sexual appetites of others. Derived from Greek *erastes* (lover) and *philia* (attachment, attraction).

> *The Democrat asserted that most Republicans are **erastophiliacs** because they realize that their own sex lives are too boring to talk about.*

erotauxesis (*erō*-tôks-Ē-sis): an increase in sexual appetite. Derived from Greek *eros* (desire, sexual love) and *auxesis* (increase).

> *The more financial and political power some men acquire, the more they experience **erotauxesis**, appearing to require ever-increasing opportunities for sex.*

erotic inertia (i-ROT-ik ĭ-NUR-shə): a condition in which people are unable to initiate or maintain sexual activity under normally favorable circumstances. Derived from Greek *eros* (sexual love) and Latin *inertia* (unskillfulness, inactivity, laziness).

> *Clyde's **erotic inertia** endangered his relationship with his sexually energetic wife.*

erotogenesis (i-*ro*-tə-JEN-i-sis): the creation of lust. Derived from Greek *eros* (desire, sexual love) and *gignesthai* (to be born).

> *The high school principal asserted that female students are asked not to wear skirts that go above their knees, lest the students should encourage **erotogenesis**.*

erotogenic (i-*ro*-tə-JEN-ik): promoting lust. Derived from Greek *eros* (desire, sexual love) and *gignesthai* (to be born).

> *In the 1950s, many social critics disapproved of rock 'n' roll because they viewed it as **erotogenic**.*

erotographomania (i-*ro*-tə-graf-ə-MĀN-ē-ə): arousal from writing love poems or letters. Derived from Greek *eros* (desire, sexual love), *graphein* (to write), and *mania* (madness, craving).

> *We did not appreciate the extent of our uncle's **erotographomania** until we discovered copies of his three thousand love letters.*

erotolalia (i-*rotō*-LĀL-lē-ə): the use of sexually explicit talk to express sexual interest or to increase arousal during loveplay. Derived from Greek *eros* (sexual love) and *lalia* (talk, conversation, chatter).

> *Many men and women whose language is quite "clean" at work find **erotolalia** extremely stimulating in the bedroom.*

erotomania (i-*rotō*-MĀN-ē-ə): a psychiatric term referring either to (i) a preoccupation with sexual thoughts and fantasies, or to (ii) a compulsive, insatiable desire for sexual activity. Derived from Greek *eros* (desire, sexual love) and *mania* (madness, craving).

The historic Casanova and the legendary Don Juan were given to **erotomania**.

erotomaniac (i-*rotō*-MĀN-ē-ak): a person who has an excessive desire for, or interest in, sex. Derived from Greek *eros* (desire, sexual love) and *mania* (madness, craving).

To an **erotomaniac**, *sex is an all-consuming interest.*

erotopath (i-*rotō*-path): a person having "abnormal" sexual desires. Derived from Greek *eros* (desire, sexual love) and *pathos* (experience, emotion, passion, suffering).

We won't say that George was an **erotopath**, *but he liked to have sex on top of the burners of a stove—while they were on.*

erotophilia (i-*rotō*-FIL-ē-ə): a condition in which people feel comfortable with, and positive about, their sexual nature and responses. Derived from Greek *eros* (sexual love) and *philia* (attachment, attraction).

Bobby and Cindy regarded their sex lives as ideal, and enjoyed their **erotophilia**.

erotophobia (i-*rotō*-FŌB-ē-ə): a morbid dislike or fear of sex. Derived from Greek *eros* (desire, sexual love) and *phobos* (fear).

Some persons who are taught that sex is "dirty" come to suffer from **erotophobia**.

esodophobia (e-sodō-FŌB-ē-ə): a morbid fear of one's first act of intercourse, a word especially applied to women. Derived from Greek *eisodos* (a coming in) and *phobos* (fear).

Because Becky was only sixteen and feared that she was not emotionally prepared for sexual intimacy, she experienced **esodophobia** *the night her boyfriend proposed that they begin to have sex.*

eugenicon (ū-*jen*-i-KON): in sexual intercourse, the mental image created by one of the participants of a different partner regarded as more desirable to increase the pleasure of the act.

Men who slept with Marilyn Monroe most likely felt no need for a **eugenicon** *at the time.*

evirate (ēvī′ rət): an archaic term for a man who has been emasculated;

also a term applied to a man who is under the delusion that he has turned into a woman. Derived from Greek *ex* (out of) and Latin *vir* (man).

> *The conservative insisted that many "radical feminists" want to transform the American male into an* **evirate.**

exogamy (eks-SOG-ə-mē): the custom of marrying outside one's tribe, family, clan, religion, or other social unit. Derived from Greek *exo* (outside, from) and *gamos* (marriage).

> *Some people have argued that* **exogamy** *can be socially beneficial to the extent that it can reduce prejudice and insularity.*

exophilia (eks-sō-FIL-ē-ə): sexual arousal from the unusual or the bizarre. Derived from Greek *ex* (out of) and *philia* (attachment, attraction).

> *The pornographer Larry Flynt has insisted that his sexual tastes are "vanilla," falling quite short of* **exophilia.**

F

faunadestia (fä-nə-DES-tē-ə): the tendency to feel embarrassment from seeing animals either have sex or scratch their genitals. Derived from the Latin *Fauna* (Roman god of nature and fertility) and *modestia* (shyness).

> *When Laura saw the two dogs copulating, she froze from* **faunadestia.**

faunoiphilia (fä-nō-i-FIL-ē-ə): an attraction to, and excitement from, watching animals (especially dogs) have sex. Derived from Latin *Fauna* (Roman god of nature and fertility), Greek *koinonia* (copulation), and Greek *philia* (attachment, attraction).

> *My nephew was stunned to hear the dog breeder frankly admit that he felt driven to that profession by his* **faunoiphilia.**

felching: the practice of licking or sucking semen from the anus or vagina; at times the term for the practice of inserting animals into the anus or vagina.

> *After the Republican candidate accused his Democrat opponent of fleecing the public and* **felching** *his perverted friends, we knew that he had completely given up on getting any of the gay vote.*

fellate (fə-LĀT): to perform oral sex on the penis. Derived from Latin *fellare* (to suck).

> *We couldn't believe that the prostitute* **fellated** *the young man in broad daylight on the street corner.*

fellatio (fə/fe-LĀ-shē-ō): oral sex on the penis. Derived from Latin *fellare* (to suck).

*Because of Bill Clinton's affair with Monica Lewinsky, many parents felt impelled to discuss the embarrassing topic of **fellatio** with their children.*

fellator (fə/fe-LĀ-tor): a male who performs oral sex on a penis. Derived from Latin *fellare* (to suck).

*The religious conservative asserted that Americans will never elect a **fellator** to the White House, though some Americans (especially Democrats) have elected a few to the U.S. House of Representatives.*

femandrism (fe-man-DRIZ-əm): effeminate characteristics in a man. Derived from Latin *femina* (woman) and Greek *aner, andr-* (man).

*The minister asserted that we need men to be men and women to be women, not men overtaken by **femandrism** or women who look as if they could be professional linebackers.*

femormia (fə/fe-MORM-ē-ə): sexual pleasure from seeing or touching a female's thigh. Derived from Latin *femur* (thigh) and Greek *horme* (desire, impulse).

*The bouncer told us that it is difficult to prevent men with **femormia** from touching the thighs of lap dancers.*

ficaro (fĭ-KARO): a house of prostitution, brothel, especially one catering to those with unusual tastes. Derived from Latin *ficus* (fig) and its allusion to sexual intercourse.

The Tom Cruise character in the movie Risky Business *allowed his home to be turned into a **ficaro**.*

flaccilation (flak-si-LĀ-shən): the waning of sexual vitality in males. Derived from Latin *flaccus* (flabby).

*Madonna presents herself as a woman who demands attention from men of great sexual energy, not men undergoing **flaccilation**.*

flatuphilia (flach-ə-FIL-ē-ə): arousal from partner's passing gas. Derived from Latin *flatus* (an act of blowing or breaking wind).

*Because of Poindexter's **flatuphilia**, his wife would eat as many beans as possible before they made love.*

fleshy excrescence (FLESH-ē ik-SKRES-əns): an old term for clitoris. An excrescence is a natural appendage. Derived from Latin *excrescere* (to grow out).

*The porn star Vanessa Del Rio was known for her remarkably large **fleshy excrescence**.*

formicophilia (for-mi-kə-FĒL-ē-ə): a species of zoophilia (*see entry*) in which people depend for arousal on the sensations produced by small creatures, such as ants, other insects, and snails, crawling or nibbling genitalia or nipples. Derived from Latin *formica* (ant) and Greek *philia* (attachment, attraction).

*We had no idea that Daniel had **formicophilia** until we discovered that he had smeared honey all over his genitalia before rolling over several ant hills.*

fratilagnia (frat-i-LAG-nē-ə): arousal from sex with one's brother. Derived from Latin *frater* (brother) and Greek *lagneia* (lust).

*The social critic submitted that, while incest is an important topic for public discussion, various forms of incestuous temptations and practices, including **fratilagnia**, should not be treated as sources of TV entertainment.*

frictation (frik-TĀ-shən): a homosexual practice in which two males rub against each other while in a face-to-face position; called **tribadism** in lesbians. Derived from Latin *fricare* (to rub).

*When the wrestling coach learned that a few of his wrestlers were engaging in **frictation**, he prohibited all his wrestlers from practicing their moves without adult supervision.*

frigoamia (frig-ə-AM-ē-ə): the uncomplaining acceptance of a woman's frigidity. Derived from Latin *frigor* (cold) and *amicus* (friendly).

*When we learned that the politician's wife had been frigid for several years, we were surprised by his **frigoamia**—until we learned of his ongoing infidelities.*

frottage (fru-TÄZH): the practice of rubbing one's genitalia against people in crowded surroundings, such as subways, buses, and elevators, for sexual gratification. The persons engaged in the practice are usually men, and the objects of their attention are usually women. Derived from the French for "rubbing."

*The young woman would always carry several packages on the elevator to minimize her risk of **frottage**.*

frotteur (fru-TUR): a male who likes to rub against women, as in crowded places. Derived from French *frotter* (to rub).

*Jason didn't want Leigh to ride the subway because he did not want a **frotteur** to rub against his wife's butt.*

furtling: a form of entertainment popular during the Victorian period in which people would use their fingers to represent genitals and breasts in cut-outs of sketches or photographs. A popular sketchbook used for furtling contained sketches of ordinary people unknowingly or unintentionally exposing themselves to others, as when a woman was depicted as having the front of her skirt bitten out by a horse.

*Robert's book on **furtling** contained directions on how to hold the fingers behind the holes.*

G

galateism (*gal*-ə-TĒ-izəm): a tendency to fall in love with, or develop a sexual interest in, figurines or statues of young women. Derived from *Galatea*, the statue with which Pygmalion fell in love.

*When Eddie began enthusiastically licking the figurines, Wally called him a creep for indulging in **galateism**.*

gamomania (gam-ə-MĀN-ē-ə): compulsion to make outlandish marriage proposals. Derived from Greek *gamos* (marriage) and *mania* (madness, craving).

*We knew that Mookie was suffering from **gamomania** when he wrote a letter to Idi Amin asking the former dictator of Uganda to marry him.*

gamonomania (gam-ə-nō-MĀN-ē-ə): an extreme desire to marry, or a morbid preoccupation with marriage. Derived from Greek *gamos* (marriage) and *mania* (madness, craving).

*We were concerned that Sheila's **gamonomania** would lead her to marry too hastily.*

gamophobia (gam-ə-FŌB-ē-ə): a morbid fear of marriage. Derived from Greek *gamos* (marriage) and *phobos* (fear).

*By getting married, actor Warren Beatty disabused many people of the idea that he was suffering from terminal **gamophobia**.*

gemellipara (jə-me/mə-LIP-ə-rə): a woman who has given birth to twins. Derived from Latin *gemellus* (twin).

*The **gemellipara** was proud of both twins.*

genasthenia (jen-ə-STHĒN-ē-ə): the absence of sexual vitality. Derived from Greek *genos* (race, kind, sex) and *asthenes* (weak, literally, "without strength").

Because of the deterioration of Elmer's physical health, he experienced genasthenia, which disappointed his wife, who was used to a robust sex life.

geneclexis (jen-ə-KLEK-sis): selection of a wife for physical or sexual appeal, as opposed to her intellectual qualities. Derived from Greek *genos* (sex, birth, origin) and *eklegein* (to select), as in "eclectic."
The model's husband insisted that he picked his wife for numerous reasons, none related to geneclexis.

genicon (JEN-ə-kon): a mental image of a sexual partner different from one's current actual partner held in one's mind during sex to increase pleasure. The imagined partner can be real. Derived from Greek *genos* (sex, birth, origin) and *eikon* (image, figure). (*See* **eugenicon.**)
Michelle would watch a Richard Gere movie before having sex with her husband to inspire a genicon.

genitive case: Occurs in Shakespeare's *The Merry Wives of Windsor*. An intentional and humorous malapropism for the vagina, as a house for the generative organs. Derived from Latin *genetivus* (of birth, generation).

genolimia (*jen-ə-LIM/LĒM-ē-ə*): starvation of sexual appetite. Derived from Greek *genos* (race, kind, sex) and *limos* (hunger).
Because Christopher was given solitary confinement, he experienced genolimia.

genopast (JENə-past): a person with unconventional or even "abnormal" sexual tastes and interests. Derived from Greek *genos* (race, kind, sex) and *paizo* (to play).
In the movie Pay It Forward, *Kevin Cline gave a thrashing to a middle-aged genopast who took a sexual interest in the character played by Haley Joel Osment.*

genophobia (*jen-ə-FŌB-ē-ə*): a morbid fear of sex. Derived from Greek *genos* (race, sex, kind) and *phobos* (fear).
Whenever Dr. Ruth would appear on David Letterman's show, he would seem to be overcome by genophobia.

genosthenia (je-nə-S*TH*ĒN-e-ə): male sexual vitality or potency. Derived from Greek *genos* (race, kind, sex) and *sthenos* (strong).
The movie character Austin Powers, satirically modeled on the lady-killer James Bond, prides himself on his genosthenia.

genuphallation (jen-yə-fal-LĀ-shən): the insertion and thrusting of the penis between the knees of the partner. Derived from Latin *genu* (knee) and Greek *phallos* (penis).

> *Bob and Sherry engaged in **genuphallation** partly because Bob liked knees, and partly because they wanted to reduce the risk of pregnancy.*

genuphile (jen-yə-FĪL): a person attracted to knees. Derived from Latin *genu* (knee) and Greek *philia* (attachment, attraction).

> *The nun would always wear dresses that would completely cover her knees to avoid arousing any **genuphiles**.*

gerafavic (jerə-FĀV-ik): having a sexual preference for older women. Derived from Greek *geras* (old age) and Latin *faveo* (to favor).

> *We weren't sure whether our friend's interest in older women was financial, or whether his sexual tastes were **gerafavic**.*

gerontolagnia (*jeron*-tə-LAG-nē-ə): unusually strong sexual desire felt by elderly persons, especially men. Derived from Greek *geron* (old man) and *lagneia* (lust).

> *Because many people are not used to accepting the idea that many elderly persons can enjoy an extremely vital sex life, manifestations of **gerontolagnia** disturb them.*

gerontophilia (*jeron*-tə-FIL-ē-ə): sexual attraction to elderly men. Derived from Greek *geron* (old man) and *philia* (attachment, attraction).

> *We did not learn about Lauren's **gerontophilia** until we saw her handing out her phone number to a dozen septuagenarians at the bingo parlor.*

glutolatry (glōō-TOL-ə-trē): excessive interest in the female buttocks. Derived from Greek *gloutos* (buttocks) and *latreia* (service, worship).

> *A man's **glutolatry** does not give him a right to pinch a woman's buttocks.*

glutomania (*glōōtō*-MĀN-ē-ə): the highest possible attraction to the female buttocks, even stronger than **glutolatry** (*see entry*). Derived from Greek *gloutos* (buttocks) and *mania* (madness, craving).

> *The lecher had a weakness for **glutomania**, manifesting itself in his interest in things as refined as ballet and as coarse as pornographic movies, including those with such vulgar titles as* The Ass Masters.

glutophilia (glōōtō-FIL-ē-ə): a mild attraction to the female buttocks. Derived from Greek *gloutos* (buttocks) and *philia* (attachment, attraction).

*Because of Justin's **glutophilia**, he encouraged his wife to wear tight pants.*

gomphipothic (gom-fi-POTH-ik): sexually aroused by seeing beautiful teeth. Derived from Greek *gomphios* (molar tooth) and *pothos* (fond desire).
*So **gomphipothic** was my dentist that he would use dental ads as an aphrodisiac.*

gonyphilous (gə-NIF-ə-ləs): sexually attracted to knees. Derived from Greek *gony* (knee) and *philein* (to love).
*The **gonyphilous** exercise instructor would always incorporate squats into female bodybuilding routines so that he could get a good view of the women's knees.*

goy toy: a slang term for an uncircumcised penis. Derived from a Yiddish expression for "gentile."
*To shock her parents, who were Orthodox Jews, Beth told them that she liked to play with **goy toys**.*

gravida (graˊidə): a pregnant woman. Derived from Latin *gravidus* (pregnant), from *gravis* (heavy).
*Although some men are sexually aroused by pregnant women, other men are not at all attracted to **gravidas**.*

gravidity (grə-VID-it-ē): pregnancy. Derived from Latin *gravidus*, from *gravis* (heavy).
*The conservative asserted that, while only individuals can become pregnant, **gravidity** has social implications.*

Great Imitator: a common name for syphilis because many of its symptoms, when viewed separately, could indicate several different nonsyphilitic infections. More recently, chlamydia, the most common sexually transmissible disease in the United States, has been given the title.
*When our friend told us that he had acquired the **Great Imitator**, we assumed that he meant chlamydia, only because it is much more common than syphilis in the United States.*

gregomulcia (greg-ə-MUL-sē-ə): a woman's desire to be fondled in front of others, especially men. Derived from Latin *grex* (herd or crowd) and *mulceo* (to stroke, touch).
*The woman's attraction to orgies was due not to voyeurism but to **gregomulcia**, since she was an exhibitionist.*

Griselda complex: the reluctance of a father to give up his daughter to another man. American psychiatrist James Putnam coined the term from the name of a virtuous heroine in medieval romances.

*When Sheri's father refused to give her away at the wedding, we learned about his **Griselda complex**.*

gross indecency: a nineteenth-century British legal term for "anal intercourse."

*Oscar Wilde was accused of **gross indecencies** during his trial.*

gunsel (GUN-səl): slang for "a young male homosexual," especially a **catamite** (*see entry*). Derived probably from Yiddish *genzel* (gosling). The term has other slang meanings, such as "a young, naïve, or stupid person," "a treacherous person," and "a gunman." Author Dashiell Hamett described a young homosexual gunman in *The Maltese Falcon* as a "gunsel," which most readers interpreted as "gunman," and that secondary meaning is now also attached to the word.

*"I'd prefer that my sexually conservative constituents not know that my son is a **gunsel**," said the nervous politician.*

gymnographephilia (*jim*-nə-gra-fə-FIL-ē-ə): the desire for collecting and displaying scantily clad women ("pin-up girls"). Derived from Greek *gymnos* (nude), *graphe* (writing), and *philia* (attachment, attraction).

*Anyone who has seen calendars in the garages of car mechanics knows that **gymnographephilia** is common among such people.*

gymnogynomania (*jim*-nə-gīnə/jina-MĀN-ē-ak): an inordinate desire to look at naked women. Derived from Greek *gymnos* (naked), *gune, gyn-* (woman), and *mania* (madness, craving).

*His **gymnogynomania** drove the young student to bore a peep hole through the girls' locker room at school.*

gymnophallation (*jim*-nə-fal-LĀ-shən): sexual intercourse with a naked (or condomless) penis. Derived from Greek *gymnos* (naked), *phallos* (penis), and *-tion* (suffix denoting abstract nouns).

*The prostitute refused to engage in **gymnophallation** because of medical concerns.*

gymnophallic (*jim*-nə-FAL-ik): involving, or pertaining to, a naked or condomless penis. Derived from Greek *gymnos* (naked) and *phallos* (penis).

*Neil's mother cautioned him against having **gymnophallic** intercourse.*

gymnophallus (*jim*-nə-FAL-us): a naked or condomless penis.

*Greg told Jeremiah, his son, that his **gymnophallus** should always have a raincoat before entering new territory.*

gymnophobia (*jim*-nə-FŌB-ē-ə): an irrational fear of naked people. Derived from Greek *gymnos* (naked) and *phobos* (fear).

*Ancient Jews had **gymnophobia** compared with the ancient Greeks, who often celebrated the naked body.*

gymnophoria (*jim*-nə-FŌR-ē-ə): the sensation or illusion of being naked when one is not, as when a woman is ogled by a lecher. Derived from Greek *gymnos* (naked, bare) and *pherein* (to bear).

*When Harry ogled Sharon, she experienced **gymnophoria**, causing her to blush.*

gymnoscopia (*jim*-nə-SKŌP-ē-ə): the viewing of a naked body. Derived from Greek *gymnos* (naked) and *skopein* (to see or observe).

*The sociologist asserted that some forms of **gymnoscopia**, such as erotic dancing at "gentlemen's clubs," are more acceptable than other forms, such as the practice of Peeping Toms.*

gymnothesaurist (*jim*-nə-thi-SÄR-əs): a male who has collected a treasure of pictures of naked women. Derived from Greek *gymnos* (naked) and *thesaurus* (treasure).

*Christopher had a collection of naked female images that was so extensive that he became the most famous **gymnothesaurist** in Ohio.*

gynacme (ji/gī-NAK-mē): the female orgasm. Derived from Greek *gune*, *gyn-* (woman) and *akme* (top, highest point).

*Men who easily induce **gynacmes** in most of their partners usually feel proud.*

gynaecomorph (ji/gə/gī-NĒKə-morf): a male resembling a female in appearance. Derived from Greek *gyne*, *gyn-* (woman) and *-morphos* (form, shape).

*While some people think that singer David Bowie appears androgynous, others think that he looks like a **gynaecomorph**.*

gynander (ji/gī-NAN-der): a mannish woman. Derived from Greek *gune*, *gyn-* (woman) and *andr-* (man).

*Because many men strongly prefer that women be feminine, they are liable to make negative remarks about **gynanders**.*

gynecentric (ji/gī-nə-SEN-trik): centering one's energy and thought on women. Derived from Greek *gune*, *gyn-* (women) and Greek *kentron* (center of a circle).

*The old lecher was too **gynecentric** to have any hobbies but sex.*

gyneclast (gī/ji-nə-KLAST): a man who is extremely successful with women; a "lady killer." Derived from Greek *gune, gyn-* (woman) and *klastes* (breaker).

The literary character of James Bond, surrounded by beautiful women overcome by their attraction to him, was quite the gyneclast.

gynecomania (ji/gī-ne-kō-MĀN-ē-ə): excessive libido in the heterosexual male. Derived from Greek *gynaiko-* (woman) and *mania* (madness, craving).

Eric and Stan were so overpowered by their gynecomania that they propositioned all the school's cheerleaders at one time.

gynecomastia (ji/gī-ne-kō-MAST-ē-ɔ): a male's condition of having enlarged breasts, caused by fatty deposits and sometimes occurring in eunuchs or men being treated with female hormones to arrest prostate cancer. Derived from Greek *gune, gyn-* (woman) and *mastos* (breast).

The drag queen deliberately took female hormones to produce gynecomastia.

gynecomimetic (ji/gī-ne-kō-mi-MET-ik): pertaining to the impersonation of females. Derived from Greek *gynaiko-* (pertaining to a woman) and *mimesis*, from *mimeisthai* (to imitate).

When Laura entered the drag show by mistake, she fell into an ungovernable rage, in which she called the performers "gynecomimetic sodomites."

gynecothalpos (ji/gī-ne-kō-THAL-pus): the warmth of a woman's body. Derived from Greek *gynaiko-* (pertaining to a woman) and *thalpos* (warmth).

After the senator's wife caught him in bed with another woman, he said, almost indignantly, "I will not apologize for desiring gynecothalpos."

gynecozygous (ji/gī-ne-kō-ZĪ-gus): seeking the company of females, as applied to lesbians. Derived from Greek *gune, gyn-* (woman) and *zygon* (a yoke, pair), as in "azygous socks" (unpaired).

Even though depictions of lesbian relationships have become increasingly common in TV and movies, some people were surprised that in 2001 Steven Spielberg's wife played a gynecozygous woman.

gynelimia (ji/gī-nə-LIM-ē-ə): hunger for females, as after sequestration from them. Derived from Greek *gyn-* (woman) and *limos* (hunger).

Because Leonard had been in prison for three years, we could easily understand his running to bars to satisfy his gynelimia.

gynelimous (gī/ji-nə-LIM-us): hungry for female companionship or intimacy. Derived from Greek *gyn-* (woman) and *limos* (hunger).

*Nico was too **gynelimous** to remain unmarried through his thirties.*

gyneloph (gī/ji/gi-nə-LOF): female pubic hair. Derived from Greek *gyn-* (woman) and *lophos* (tuft).

The magazine Playboy *originally did not show pictures of a woman's **gyneloph** until such pictures gained a wider degree of acceptance among the public.*

gynelophilous (gī/ji-nə-LOF-ə-lus): especially fond of female pubic hair. Derived from Greek *gyn-* (woman), *lophos* (tuft), and *philein* (to love).

*The **gynelophilous** adolescent collected close-up photographs of naked women's crotches.*

gynephonia (gī/ji-nə-FŌN-ē-ə): effeminate voice in a male. Derived from Greek *gyn-* (woman) and *phone* (sound, voice).

*While many men may dislike Richard Simmons's **gynephonia**, he has doubtless helped many people.*

gynephronate (gī/ji-nə-FRŌ-nāt): to have sexual thoughts about women. Derived from Greek *gyn-* (woman) and *phren* (mind).

*Our health teacher told us that most male adolescents will **gynephronate** at least occasionally, if not a great deal more often.*

gynesadism (gī/ji-nə-SĀ-dizəm): the tendency to derive sexual pleasure from inflicting cruelty on females. Derived from Greek *gyn-* (woman) and *sadism* (from Marquis de Sade [1740–1814], an aristocratic Parisian whose life and writings centered on sexual cruelty).

There is a violent scene in the movie Body Double *that could excite only someone given over to **gynesadism**.*

gynetrichosis (gī/ji-nə-tri-KŌ-sis): excessive growth of hair on a female. Derived from Greek *gyn-* (woman) and *thrix* (hair).

*The **gynetrichosis** besetting Robert's mother was so serious that she believed that the best way for her to make a living was to perform as a bearded lady in a circus.*

gynonudomania (ji/gī-nə-nōō-dō-MĀN-ē-ə): a strong desire to expose a woman's body, as by tearing off her clothes. Derived from Greek *gune, gyn-* (woman), Latin *nudus* (naked), and Greek *mania* (madness, craving).

Many people are concerned that men who have been imprisoned for years might become so sexually desperate when they leave prison as to endanger women by yielding to **gynonudomania**.

gynophelimity (ji/gī-nof-ə-LIM-i-tē): the ability of a female to give sexual satisfaction. Derived from Greek *gyn-* (woman) and *ophelimos* (useful, helpful).

The feminist condemned those men who regard women only for their **gynophelimity**.

gynophilia (ji/gī-nə-FIL-ē-ə): love of a woman, whether by a member of either sex. Derived from Greek *gyn-* (woman) and *philia* (attachment, attraction).

When the psychiatrist was discovered having sex with one of his patients, he asked why he should be punished for **gynophilia**.

gynophobia (ji/gī-nə-FŌB-ē-ə): morbid fear of women. Derived from Greek *gune, gyn-* (woman) and *phobos* (fear).

Although some gay and heterosexual men may have **gynophobia***, it is inaccurate to think that gay men generally have that fear.*

gynoscopia (ji/gī-nə-SKŌP-ē-ə): the viewing of a naked body, especially by a staring man. Derived from Greek *gymnos* (naked) and *skopein* (to see, observe).

We asked Jennifer not to take the stripping job if **gynoscopia** *discomfits her.*

H

halitalagnia (hal-i-tə-LAG-nē-ə): loss of sexual desire or potency during sex because of the bad breath of one's partners. Derived from Latin *halitus* (exhalation), Greek *a-* (without), and Greek *lagneia* (lust).

If his wife had better dietary habits, and had brushed her teeth before having sex, Benny would not have succumbed to **halitalagnia**.

hapalophallia (hap-ə-lō-FAL-lē-ə): the condition of having a soft and nonerectible male organ. Derived from Greek *hapalos* (soft) and *phallos* (penis).

The senator refused to pay the prostitute because his **hapalophallia** *disabled her from consummating her services.*

haphemania (haf-ə-MĀN-ē-ə): (i) a strong desire to be touched or fondled; (ii) a strong desire to touch someone, especially a man's desire to touch a woman. Derived from Greek *haphe* (a touch) and *mania* (madness, craving).

*Because of Dobie's desire for Thalia and her **haphemania**, the two were constantly touching.*

haphephilia (haf-ə-FIL-ē-ə): the desire to be touched by a member of the opposite sex. Derived from Greek *haphe* (a touch) and *philia* (attachment, attraction).

*When Lucy was discovered with seven men in her bed, she said that she had felt overpowered by **haphephilia**.*

haphephobia (haf-ə-FŌB-ē-ə): the fear of being touched, especially a woman's fear that she will be touched by a repellent man. Derived from Greek *haphe* (a touch) and *phobos* (fear).

*Any woman with **haphephobia** has no business stripping at a bar with liberal touching policies.*

haploist (HAP-lō-ist): a person who believes sexual intercourse should be as brief as possible and without expressions of love, embraces, or affection. Derived from *haplous* (single, "of one fold").

*He was a **haploist** who believed that sex should be served like fast food— with great speed and no emotion.*

haptepronia (hap-tə-PRŌN-ē-ə): the condition of being favorably disposed toward romantic advances, especially from strangers. Derived from Greek *haptein* (to fasten) and Latin *pronus* (inclined, well disposed).

*Her **haptepronia** made her especially attractive to sexually desperate males.*

haptevoluptas (hap-tə-va-LUP-təs): someone extremely pleasant to touch, hold, or fondle. Derived from Greek *haptein* (to fasten) and Latin *voluptas* (pleasure). (*See also* **evancalous**.)

*The lecherous actor asserted that he has always been unable to resist a **haptevoluptas**.*

harpaxophilia (har-paks-ō-FIL-ē-ə): arousal from being raped or robbed. Derived from Greek *harpax* (robber) and *philia* (attachment, attraction).

*We did not learn about Michelle's **harpaxophilia** until we found out that she winked at the robber and gave him her phone number.*

hebephilia (heb-ə-FIL-ē-ə): male homosexual attraction to teenaged boys. Derived from Greek *hebe* (youth) and *philia* (attachment, attraction).
*In ancient Greece **hebephilia** was fairly common, but it was often part of a relationship in which the older males would instruct the younger ones in different subjects.*

hedonophobia (hē-don-ō-FŌB-ē-ə): a morbid or an irrational fear of pleasure. Derived from Greek *hedone* (pleasure) and *phobos* (fear).
*We were not sure whether Jennifer's avoidance of sex stemmed more from erotophobia, or from **hedonophobia**.*

hedralingus (hed-rə-LING-us): the practice of licking the anus. Derived from the Greek *hedra* (seat) and Latin *lingere* (to lick).
*In the 1960s performing a "brown job" referred to **hedralingus**.*

Hellenic love: archaic term meaning "male homosexuality." Derived from the practice of homosexuality in ancient Greek (*Hellenic*) culture.
*The pianist Liberace once sued someone for asserting that he practiced **Hellenic love**.*

hemerotism (hem-ə-ROT-izəm): erotic daydreaming. Derived from Greek *hemera* (day) and *eros* (sexual love).
*The nun who was our teacher tried to keep the male students so mentally and physically active that they had no time for **hemerotism** or any other "impure thoughts."*

hemeuner (hə-MOO-ner): a man either who is potent only during the daytime, or who prefers sex during the day. Derived from Greek *hemera* (day) and *eune* (bed).
*The **hemeuner** told his wife that he was sorry, but that he could not participate in lovemaking, since it was already nightfall.*

hereism (HERə-izəm): marital faithfulness. Derived from *Hera*, the Greek goddess of women and marriage.
*While no one should expect people to be perfect, it makes sense to defend **hereism** as an ideal worth taking seriously.*

hermaphrodite (hər-MAF-rə-*dīt*): someone with both ovaries and testes. There are different forms of hermaphroditism. A person with the bilateral form has an ovary and a testicle on each side of the body, while a person with the unilateral form has both an ovary and testicle on one side and either an ovary or a testicle on the other side. A pseudohermaphrodite (a false one) may have either ovaries or testes and external genitalia of the other sex, with other sexual characteristics of males and females. Conventionally, a person will be considered male if the gonads are testes, or female if the gonads are ovaries, regardless of the external genitalia. Derived from the name of the mythological son of Hercules and Aphrodite (*Hermaphroditos*) who became joined in body with Salmacis.

> *Although the character played by Hilary Swank in* Boys Don't Cry *was not a true **hermaphrodite** but a woman who felt fulfilled living as a man, the character was killed because she was different in ways that made insecure persons feel threatened.*

heterocoitus (*het*-ə-rō-KŌ-i-tus): sexual intercourse between members of opposite sexes. Derived from Greek *heteros* (other) and Latin *coitus* (intercourse).

> *The sexologist insisted that most acts of **heterocoitus** have nothing to do with procreation, but everything to do with pleasure and the release of stress and tension.*

heterodromia (*het*-ə-rō-DRŌM/DROM-ē-ə): female body movement in sexual intercourse in which the woman thrusts her genitalia upward as the man thrusts his downward. Derived from Greek *heteros* (other) and *dromos* (a running).

> *The porn director praised his copulators for their **heterodromia**.*

heterophilia (*het*-ə-rō-FIL-ē-ə): arousal from the opposite sex. Derived from Greek *heteros* (other) and *philia* (attachment, attraction).

> *When the pompous English professor was caught embracing one of his female students, he said, "I make no apologies for my **heterophilia**."*

heterosociality (*het*-ə-rō-sō-shē-AL-i-tē): the tendency to establish social relationships with members of the opposite sex, often not based on sexual desire. Derived from Greek *heteros* (other) and Latin *socialis* (of companionship).

> *Many women prefer the company of males, but their **heterosociality** is not based on sexual desire.*

heterovalent (*het*-ə-rō-VĀL-ənt): sexually potent or able to have sex only with someone other than one's wife. Derived from Greek *heteros* (other) and Latin *valero* (to be strong). (*See also* **uxurovalent**.)

> *The **heterovalent** man defended his marital infidelities by describing his **heterovalence** as an unfortunate medical condition.*

hidrophrodisia (hī/hi-drō-frə-DIZ-ē-ə): sexual arousal from the odor of perspiration, especially from the genitalia. Derived from the Greek *hidros* (perspiration) and *aphrodisia* (sexual pleasures).

*Brad's **hidrophrodisia** became embarrassing to on-lookers when he began salivating and panting in the co-ed sauna.*

hieroduli (HĪ-ər-ə-*dōōl*-ē): male temple prostitutes of ancient Greece, often cross-dressing priests. Derived from Greek *hieron* and *doulos* (slave).

*The religious conservative warned that, if contemporary religion becomes any more politically correct, **hieroduli** will be welcome in our churches.*

hierophilia (*hī*-ər-ə-FIL-ē-ə): arousal from sacred objects. Derived from Greek *hieros* (holy, sacred) and *philia* (attachment, attraction).

*When the religious man heard that some people are sexually aroused by the crucifix, he asserted that **hierophilia** is a perversion.*

hirsutophile (hur-SOO-tə-fīl): a person attracted to hairy men. Derived from Latin *hirsutus* (bristly, rough) and Greek *philein* (to love).

*When Sean Connery played James Bond, his hairy chest must have appealed to **hirsutophiles**.*

hodophilia (häd-ə-FIL-ē-ə): arousal from traveling. Derived from Greek *hodos* (path, road) and *philia* (attachment, attraction).

*Because of the couple's **hodophilia**, they would travel all across the country and have sex in as many states as possible.*

homilophilia (hom-i-lə-FIL-ē-ə): arousal from hearing or giving sermons. Derived from Latin *homilia* (conversation, discourse) and Greek *philia* (attachment, attraction).

*Some churchgoers given to **homilophilia** find sermons condemning sex so arousing that they feel impelled to have sex after hearing the sermons.*

homoeroticism (*hō*-mō-i-ROT-i-siz-əm): erotic interest in a person of the same sex. Derived from Greek *homo-* (same) and *eros* (sexual love).

*Some religious groups have objected to frank depictions of **homoeroticism** in the movies.*

homosexuality, facultative (FAK-əl-tā-tiv *hō*-mə-*sek*-shōō-AL-i-tē): homosexuality that does not exclude heterosexuality, as when people engage in homosexual behavior for sexual release, power, or control, as in prison. **Facultative homosexuality** is often used in contradistinction to **obligate homosexuality** (*see entry*), which leaves no option for bisexual or heterosexual bondings.

The prisoner who happened to be a psychiatrist asserted that, when he *engaged in **facultative homosexuality**, he did so as a sexual release and did not care that his sexual partner was anatomically similar.*

homosexuality, obligate (OB-li-git *hō*-mə-*sek*-shōō-AL-i-tē): exclusive homosexuality, leaving no option for heterosexual or bisexual bondings. *While there was presumably some **obligate homosexuality** in ancient Greece, many persons who engaged in homosexuality would today be considered bisexual.*

homosociality (*hō*-mə-*sō*-shē-AL-i-tē): when narrowly employed, the term describes the tendency of certain persons to socialize principally with persons of the same sex. People usually first form homosocial groups when children and adolescents. Some cultures encourage men and women to live most of their lives in segregated groups, and other cultures contain little or no homosociality. Derived from Greek *homos* (same) and Latin *socialitas* (fellowship).

*When political candidate A accuses political candidate B of favoring overt **homosociality**, political candidate A can sometimes gain a strong political advantage.*

homunculate (hə-MUNGK-yə-lāt): to try ineffectively to perform sexual intercourse with a small penis. Derived from Latin *homunic* (a miniature male organ).

*The poorly endowed former governor wanted to receive oral sex rather than to **homunculate** for reasons altogether obvious to his sexual partner.*

homunk (hō-MUNGK): a small penis. Derived from Latin *homunculus* (a diminutive of *homo*, man).

*Young men can be merciless in a locker room containing **homunks** in plain view.*

horizontalize: a slang for having sexual intercourse.

*Years ago athletes were warned against **horizontalizing** before a competition.*

hot sex values: a system of sexual values based on clear sex roles and stereotypes, a genital definition of sex, a belief in exclusive monogamy, emphasis on female premarital virginity, and patriarchy. Presumably, the expression hot sex values refers not to "hot sex" but to values that are hotly held and defended. Ironically, those persons most likely to hold hot sex values are highly unlikely to describe sex as "hot," while those persons with **cool sex values** (*see entry*) are likely sometimes to use the expression "hot sex." The situation is reminiscent of the words "esoteric" (narrowly known) and "exoteric" (widely known), since persons who know only exoteric words will not know "exoteric," and persons who know highly esoteric words may know "exoteric."

The evangelist Jerry Falwell doubtless believes in hot sex values, though he might become angry should someone tell him.

Hottentot bustle (HOT-ən-tot BUS-əl): a colloquial term for the medical condition known as **steatopygia** (fat buttocks) (*see entry*). The Hottentots of Southern Africa consider fat female buttocks sexy and beautiful.

"Thin may be in, but fat is where it's at," asserted Bertha, known for her **Hottentot bustle**.

houghmagandy (hōk-mə-GANDI): Scottish term for sexual intercourse engaged in as a pastime. Derived from *hough* (hock) and *canty* (cheerful, sprightly).

The mother told her adolescent son that there will be no **houghmagandy** *under her roof.*

humex (hūmeks): the normal lubricating secretion of the vulva. Derived from Latin *humere* (to be moist).

Because Jerry's wife was deficient in **humex**, *she found intercourse uncomfortable.*

hybristophilia (hi-bris-tə-FIL-ē-ə): an attraction to, and arousal from, being with a sexual partner known to have committed an outrage or crime, such as rape, murder, or armed robbery. Derived from the Greek *hybridzein* (to commit an outrage against someone) and *philia* (attachment, attraction).

The author of Lovemaps, *John Money, asserted that the attraction between outlaws Bonnie and Clyde, and between Charles Manson and his "family," reflected* **hybristophilia**.

hygrophilematous (hī-*grof*-i-LEM-ə-tus): relating to "wet" kisses, or fond of "wet" kisses. Derived from Greek *hygros* (wet) and *philema* (a kiss).

The young man enjoyed the **hygrophilematous** *interaction between actresses Neve Campbell and Denise Richards in the 1998 movie* Wild Things.

hygrophilia (*hi*-grə-FIL-ē-ə): attraction to, or arousal from, contact with any bodily secretions, including saliva, urine, feces, semen, and mammary secretions. Derived from Greek *hygros* (wet, moist) and *philia* (attachment, attraction).

We knew that Thelma Lou was given to **hygrophilia** *when, after* *instructing several persons to urinate and defecate on her, she shouted out, "It's time for the lactators."*

hymenomania (*hī*-men-ə-MĀN-ē-ə): an inordinate desire to deflower a virgin. Derived from Greek *hymen* (the virginal membrane) and *mania* (madness, craving).

*The group of adolescent males who competed for seducing virgins seemed proud of their **hymenomania**.*

hymenopenthy (hī-men-ə-PEN-*thē*): depression caused by loss of virginity. Derived from *Hymen* (Greek god of marriage but also the name of the fold of mucous membrane partly closing the orifice of the vagina) and *pentheo* (to mourn for).

*Because Wilma lost her virginity while she was intoxicated and to a boy she hardly knew, she fell into **hymenopenthy**.*

hypercosmosis (*hī*-pər-koz-MŌ-sis): the excessive but not necessarily unbecoming development of secondary sex characteristics in females. Derived from Greek *huper* (over, beyond), *kosmeo* (decorate), and *-osis* (suffix denoting a condition).

*Because of Britney's **hypercosmosis**, she looked twenty even when she was fourteen.*

hypergenitalism (*hī*-pər-JEN-i-tl-izəm): overdevelopment of the genitals. Derived from Greek *huper* (over, beyond) and *gignere* (to beget).

*Wayne's **hypergenitalism** led him to try erotic dancing at some sleazy clubs.*

hyperphilia (*hī*-pər-FIL-ē-ə): compulsive desire for sex. Derived from Greek *huper* (over, beyond) and *philia* (attachment, attraction).

*The young man asserted that **hyperphilia** is more common among men than women because men have much more testosterone.*

hyphephilia (*hī*-fə-FIL-ē-ə): derivation of sexual pleasure from touching certain surfaces, such as velvet. Derived from Greek *hype* (web) and *philein* (to love).

*The expression on Barry's face as he was stroking velvet led us to believe that he is affected by **hyphephilia**.*

hypogenitalism (*hī*-pō-JEN-i-tl-izəm): underdevelopment of the genitals. Derived from Greek *hypo* (under, beneath) and *gignere* (to beget).

*Johnny likes to make fun of his **hypogenitalism**, saying that his sexual partners need tweezers to manipulate his phallus.*

hypolibida (*hī*-pō-li-BĪ-də): a female with an unusually low sex drive. Derived from Greek *hypo* (under, beneath), Latin *libido* (desire, lust), and *-a* (feminine suffix).

> *Because Bill is intensely sexual, he would do well to avoid marrying a* ***hypolibida.***

hypolibidus (*hī*-pō-li-BĪ-dus): a male with an unusually low sex drive. Derived from Greek *hypo* (under, beneath) and Latin *libido* (desire, lust).

> *Most people think that it must be exceedingly difficult for anyone but a* ***hypolibidus*** *to keep a vow of chastity for several years.*

hypomazia (*hī*-pō-MĀZ/MAZ-ē-ə): underdevelopment of the breasts. Derived from Greek *hypo* (under, beneath) and *mazos* (breast).

> *Many women want breast transplants because of their* ***hypomazia.***

hypomedia (*hī*-pō-MĒD-ē-ə): the condition of having an underdeveloped penis. Derived from Greek *hypo* (under, beneath) and *medos* (penis).

> *Mickey's* ***hypomedia*** *was so striking that other boys in the locker room would call him "Mr. Thimble."*

hypsilatry (hip-SIL-ə-trē): the worship or adoration of the line of cleavage of a woman's breasts, especially the upper portion visible above a décolletage. Derived from the name of the letter "Y" (upsilon) and *latreia* (worship).

> *His* ***hypsilatry*** *made it difficult for the lecher to notice anything above the shapely woman's bust line.*

I

iatronudia (ī-at-rə-NOŎD-ē-ə): a woman's pretending to be sick because she wants to disrobe in front of a doctor. Derived from Greek *iatros* (doctor).

> *When Abe learned about Mary's* ***iatronudia,*** *he sent her to the oldest doctor he could find.*

iconolagny (ī-kon-ə-LAGNĒ): sexual excitement from pictures or statues. Derived from Greek *eikon* (image) and *lagneia* (lust).

> *The psychologist asserted that, because men tend to be more visually oriented than women, they tend to experience* ***iconolagny*** *more often than women.*

idiogamist (id-ē-OG-ə-mist): a man capable of coitus only with his wife. Derived from the Greek *idios* (one's own) and *gamos* (marriage).

*The religious man affirmed that he, unlike certain sexually compulsive politicians, is an **idiogamist** and proud of it.*

idiorrhenic (id-ē-ō-RENIK): peculiar to, or definitive of, males. Derived from Greek *idios* (one's own) and *arrhen* (male).

*The feminist criticized those men who take pride in their **idiorrhenic** appendages.*

idiosyncrat (id-ē-ō-SIN-krat): a person with unconventional if not "abnormal" desires, especially sexual ones. Derived from Greek *idios* (one's own) and *synkrasis* (action of blending).

*The Democrat fund-raiser told his Hollywood audience that the Democrat tent is wide enough to fit people of all sorts, including **idiosyncrats**.*

idiothelic (id-ē-ō-thel-ik): peculiar to, or definitive to, females. Derived from Greek *idios* (one's own) and *thelys* (female).

*The smark-alecky but precocious student told the class that his goal in life is to explore with tireless assiduity **idiothelic** orifices.*

imatolibidin(ĭ-mat-ō-li-BI/BĒ-dən): an imagined liquid preparation that can supposedly arouse the libido of young women. Derived from Greek *iama* (remedy) and Latin *libido* (lust).

*The scientist said that there is no **imatolibidin** that will make an obnoxious and inconsiderate young man attractive to women.*

imparcolpia (im-par-KOLP-ē-ə): enforced virginity, as by religious vows, imprisonment, absence of sex partners, and so on. Derived from Latin *impar* (unequal, unpaired) and Greek *kolpos* (womb, breast, vagina).

*The prisoners were extremely frustrated because of their **imparcolpia**.*

imparkoinonia (im-par-koi-NŌN-ē-ə): sexual intercourse in which one partner derives much more satisfaction than the other. Derived from Latin *impar* (unequal) and Greek *koinonia* (sexual intercourse).

*Roger, who always enjoyed sex with his wife, could not understand the source of their **imparkoinonia**.*

imparlibidinous (im-par-li-BID-i-nəs): unfavorably matched in libido or sex drive, as when a husband or a wife is generally more passionate than the spouse. Derived from Latin *impar* (unequal) and *libido* (sex drive).

*President John F. Kennedy and his wife were **imparlibidinous**.*

inappetence (in-AP-pi-təns): an absence of sexual desire or libido. Derived from Latin *in-* (not) and *appetere* (to desire, long for).

The ambitious young man did not view himself as suffering from ***inappetence****, but simply saw himself as valuing other things much more highly than sex.*

incoercible apathy (*in*-kō-UR-sə-bəl AP-ə-thē): invincible female sexual indifference.

When Bertha rebuffed Reggie's advances, he was not sure whether she happened to find him unattractive, or was acting from ***incoercible apathy****.*

incubous (IN-kyə-bəs): lying upon or atop, such as the coital partner who is on top of the other. Derived from Latin *incumbare* (to lie upon).

Maria liked the ***incubous*** *position in lovemaking because it gave her more control and freedom of movement.*

incubus (IN-kyə-bəs): a medieval term for a demon that assumes the shape of a man and has intercourse with a sleeping woman. Some scholars think that belief in **incubi** might have been motivated at least partly by a desire to explain out-of-wedlock births. Derived from the Latin *incubare* (to lie down on).

When Jenna told her father that she became pregnant because of an ***incubus****, he did not take her seriously.*

indorser (in-DORSER): an obsolete slang term for the active partner in anal intercourse. Derived from Latin *in-* (upon, in) and *dorsum* (back).

Men who enjoy being ***indorsers*** *will sometimes have trouble finding women who receive people through their back doors.*

infibulation (in-fib-yə-LĀ-shən): either the sewing or the fastening of the foreskin over the penis, or the sewing of the labia minora or labia majora together, or the sewing of the scrotum around the penis. Infibulation has been used on young girls in Africa to ensure their virginity at marriage. Derived from Latin *infibulare* (to infibulate).

Many westerners consider female ***infibulation****, practiced, for example, in parts of Africa, physical abuse.*

ingressability (in-*gress*-ə-BIL-i-tē): the ability of a penis to penetrate a vagina. Derived from Latin *ingredi* (to go into).

The sex therapist stated that male impotence is only one factor influencing ***ingressability****, since there are other factors as well, including the penetrability of a woman's hymen.*

inspectionism: a psychiatric term for **voyeurism** (*see entry*). Derived from the idea of inspecting or watching.

> *When Dempster told us that his main interest was **inspectionism**, we had no idea that he was a voyeur, but thought that he was in charge of quality assurance at some factory.*

intermazium (in-ter-MĀZ/MAZ-ē-əm): the space between the female breasts. Derived from Latin *inter* (between) and Greek *mazos* (breast).

> *Dolly's breasts were so impressive that her husband rarely noticed her **intermazium**.*

introitus (in-TRŌəD-əs): body cavity, especially the vagina. Derived from a Latin word for "entrance."

> *Rudy told his daughter's fiancé that her **introitus** is off limits to him until the wedding night.*

intromission (*in*-trə-MISH-ən): insertion of the penis into the vagina during sexual intercourse. Derived from Latin *intromissus*, past particle of *intromittere* (to send or let in).

> *When Dingbang heard that it was time for the intermission, he thought the emcee said **intromission**, and was charged with committing a lewd act in public.*

inunction (in-UNGK-shən): act of rubbing ointment or lather on a person, as in preparation for close or intimate contact with another person. In the United States during the 1960s, some people had Mazola parties, in which they would undress, rub their bodies with oil, and wrestle or play on plastic sheets. Derived from past participle of Latin *inunguere* (to anoint).

> *Bob's girlfriend was a talented masseuse whose skills at **inunction** were deeply appreciated.*

invirility (in-və-RIL-i-tē): impotence. Derived from the Latin *in-* (not) and *vir* (man).

> *Because of Kato's **invirility**, he chose to masturbate his wife instead of performing intercourse.*

ipsation (ip-SĀ-shən): self-induced sexual excitement, including masturbation; an obsolete term for "autoeroticism." Derived from Latin *ipse* (self, oneself).

> *When the actor who played Pee-Wee Herman was caught practicing **ipsation** in a Florida movie theater, his career was seriously damaged.*

ipserotic (ip-se/sə-ROT-ik): focusing one's sexual attentions on one's own body. Derived from Latin *ipse* (self, oneself).

*Howard was so **ipserotic** that all he needed for sexual fulfillment was a mirror and his right hand.*

ipsithigmophilous (ip-si-thig-MOF-ə-lus): enjoying the touch of one's own body, much more common in women than men; the term can also pertain to a man's desire to watch a woman touch or handle her private parts. Derived from Latin *ipse* (self), Greek *thigma* (touch), and Greek *philein* (to love).

In the movie Body Double, *the character played by Angie Dickenson appears so **ipsithigmophilous** in a shower scene that she looks as if she's lusting after her own body.*

irrumation (i-rōo-MĀ-shən): the act of thrusting the penis into someone's mouth for oral sex. Derived from the Latin *irrumare* (to extend the penis for oral sex).

The premise of the pornographic movie Deep Throat *was that, because of an anatomical abnormality, a woman could achieve orgasm only through **irrumation**.*

irrumator (i-rōo-MĀ-tor): a male who performs the active role of insertor in fellatio (*see entry*) with another male. Derived from Latin *irrumare* (to extend the penis for oral sex).

*Because Andy was always the **irrumator** in his sexual relations with other men, he usually defined himself as essentially heterosexual.*

ischolagny (is-kō-LAG-nē): the avoidance of even the sight of women, or anything suggestive of them to suppress one's lust for them. The practice is observed by those males whose moral or religious code requires abstinence but whose sexual cravings are strong and easily aroused. Derived from Greek *ischein* (to hold, restrain) and *lagneia* (lust).

*The minister said that if we are to reduce the incidence of casual sex, we must reduce the number of co-ed dormitories at colleges and move toward **ischolagny**.*

isodromia (ī-sə-DRŌM/DROM-ē-ə): a woman's up-and-down movement during intercourse, matching the man's thrusts instead of complementing them, leading to awkward intercourse. Derived from Greek *isos* (equal) and *dromos* (running).

*Royal told Belinda that her **isodromia** is turning their sexual encounters into an arduous exercise instead of a joy.*

isomulcia (ī-sə-MUL-sē-ə): the desire to embrace or fondle a woman in the presence of a man. Derived from Greek *isos* (equal) and Latin *mulceo* (to stroke).
*Johnny's **isomulcia** led him often to fondle his girlfriend in public.*

isonogamia (ī-so-nō-GAM-ē-ə): a marriage whose participants are roughly the same age. Derived from Greek *isos* (equal) and *gamos* (marriage).
*We hope that the **isonogamia** between Heather and Brian works out well.*

isosexual (ī-sə-SEK-sho͞o-əl): an obsolete term for "homosexual." The term usually now means "pertaining to the same sex," but used to mean "a homosexual." Derived from Greek *isos* (equal).
*Thorndike is naïve and thinks that **isosexual** is a word for describing a frigid person.*

iterandria (it-ur-ANDRIA): male homosexuality. Derived from Latin *itero* (to repeat) and Greek *andr-* (man).
*Rumors about the young actor's **iterandria** have not hurt his career, partly because of his immense popularity, and partly because most of his fans believe that he is quite heterosexual.*

ithyalgia (i-thi-AL-j(ē)ə): a painful erection. Derived from Greek *ithys* (straight) and Greek *algos* (pain).
*Because of his medical condition, Rush suffered from **ithyalgia**, which made intercourse all but impossible.*

ithyphallic (*ith-ə/*i-FAL-ik): having an erect penis, a word used especially to describe statues or drawings; lustful, obscene. Derived from Greek *ithys* (straight) and *phallos* (penis). The English word is derived from a Greek word describing festivals celebrating the Greek and Roman god of revelry, Bacchus, in whose honor there were ithyphallic processions, in which artistic representations of penises were carried.
*The elderly woman was embarrassed by the **ithyphallic** statue.*

ithyphallus (ith-ə-FAL-us): an erection. Derived from Greek *ithys* (straight) and *phallos* (penis).
*Although many R-rated movies will show full frontal nudity, especially of females, they will usually avoid showing an **ithyphallus**.*

J

jactitation (jak-ti-TĀ-shən): a male's boasting that he succeeded in having sex with a particular female, whether he did or not. Derived from Latin *iactare* (to boast).

*The coach told the sexual braggart that gentlemen keep their private lives private, and do not engage in **jactitation**, possibly harming a woman's reputation just for male aggrandizement.*

Jocasta complex: morbid attachment of a mother to her own son. Derived from the classic Greek legend in which Oedipus unwittingly slew his father and unwittingly married his mother, Jocasta, who was equally ignorant of their biological relationship. When the facts became known, Jocasta hanged herself, and Oedipus tore out his own eyes.

*Because of the sexually suggestive ways in which Joan touched her son, we wondered whether she was acting out the **Jocasta complex**.*

K

kakopyge (kakō-PĪJE/PIJĒ): someone with ugly buttocks. Derived from the Greek *kakos* (bad) and *pyge* (buttocks).

*Richard Simmons has probably met a large number of **kakopyges** in his work.*

kaleidogyn (kə-LĪ-dō-jin): a beautiful woman. Derived from the Greek *kalos* (beautiful) and *gune, -gyn* (woman).

*The **kaleidogyn** understandably objected to being appreciated for only her physical beauty.*

kedavalence (ke-də-VĀL-ēns): male sexual impotence due to worry. Derived from Greek *kedos* (concern), *a* (without), Latin *valere* (to be able).

*Ricky was so worried that Lucy would discover his infidelities that he experienced **kedavalence**, temporarily disabling him from making love.*

Kegel exercises: repeated contraction and release of muscles surrounding the opening of the vagina and supporting the woman's internal organs. Developed by Dr. Alfred Kegel in 1952, the exercises reportedly are capable of not only strengthening the female orgasm but also helping prepare for childbirth, reduce urinary incontinence, and prevent prolapse of the womb.

*When Sheri became pregnant, she began to practice **Kegel exercises**.*

Kempf's disease: behavior described by American psychiatrist Edward Kempf as acute homosexual panic, stemming from fear either that the sufferers may be attacked by homosexuals, or that they may be identified as homosexual; "homosexual panic."

> *In the movie* Rebel Without A Cause, *there is a scene in a police station in which a man is depicted as displaying behavior associated with **Kempf's disease**.*

kenorgasmy (*ken*-or-GAZ-mē): a male orgasm producing some pleasure, but no ejaculate. Derived from Greek *kenos* (empty) and *orgasmos* (swelling).

> *Most producers of pornographic movies do not want **kenorgasmies** because many viewers want to see ejaculate.*

kleptolagnia (klep-tō-LAG-nē-ə): arousal from stealing. Derived from Greek *kleptein* (to steal) and *lagneia* (lust).

> *Barry stole not to get what he needed, but to satisfy his **kleptolagnia**.*

klismaphilia (klis-mə-FIL-ē-ə): sexual arousal from enemas. Derived from Greek *klisma* (enema) and *philia* (attachment, attraction).

> *We suspected Paul of **klismaphilia** when he asked the waiter to serve his wine and coffee in the bathroom, into which Paul carried a black leather bag.*

knismolagnia (nis-mə-LAG-nē-ə): arousal from tickling, or being tickled. Derived from Greek *knismos* (a tickling) and *lagneia* (lust).

> *Because of their **knismolagnia**, the two lovers would have feathers near their bed.*

koinasthenia (koi-nas-*THĒ*-nē-ə): loss of confidence and security, with restlessness and anxiety, because of self-blame for unsatisfactory sexual relations with one's spouse. Derived from Greek *koinonia* (communion, intercourse, association) and *asthenia* (lack of strength).

> *When Andy would experience **koinasthenia** because of rocky relations with Flo, he would head to his local pub.*

koinocrasia (koi-nə-CRĀ-zhə, koi-nə-CRAZ-ē-ə): sexual activities involving "normal" and "abnormal" acts. Derived from Greek *koinonia* (communion, intercourse, association) and *krasis* (a mixture).

> *When Pervis told us that his sex life was quite conventional, we knew that he was unusual enough occasionally to practice **koinocrasia**.*

kokigami (koki-GÄ-mē, kō-ki-GÄ-mē): the Japanese art of wrapping the penis in a paper costume. Derived from Japanese *koki* (cloth) and *gami* (paper).

> *Akira and Yoko liked to practice* **kokigami,** *especially when Yoko would unwrap Akira's costume to get to her "prize."*

kolpectasia (kol-pek-TĀZHA): a stretching or dilation of the vagina, as from sexual intercourse. Derived from Greek *kolpos* (womb, breast, vagina) and *ectasia* (a stretching).

> *Her gynecologist told Sarah that her* **kolpectasia** *was due to her frequent intercourse.*

kolpeuryntalgia (kol-pur-in-TAL-j(ē)ə): a vaginal pain produced by stretching to accommodate the phallus. Derived from Greek *kolpos* (womb, breast, vagina), *eurynein* (to dilate), and *algos* (pain).

> *We asked the porn star whether she ever experienced* **kolpeuryntalgia** *in her relations with Long Dong Silver.*

kolpocingulaphoria (kol-pə-sing-yə-lə-FOR-ē-ə): the sensation of having the penis tightly embraced by the vagina during intercourse, as during intercourse with a virgin. Derived from Greek *kolpos* (womb, breast), Latin *cingulum* (girdle), and Greek *pherein* (to bear).

> *Because Gloria recently gave birth, Michael could not experience* **kolpocingulaphoria** *when they had sex.*

kolpophobia (kol-po-FOB-ē-ə): fear of, or aversion to, sexual intercourse or the female sexual organs. Derived from Greek *kolpos* (womb, breast, vagina) and *phobos* (fear).

> *Since Festus wanted to enjoy sexual relations with Kitty, he agreed to undergo treatment called "systematic desensitization" to overcome his* **kolpophobia.**

kordax: a phallic dance by horned figures in the Dionysian festivals of ancient Greece. Derived from Greek *kordax* (to stake, brandish).

> *After the minister saw the Red Hot Chili Peppers' video Give It Up, he asserted that millions of Americans have come to glorify what is dangerously close to a* **kordax.**

koro (KÔ-rō): a culturally induced psychological "disorder" characterized either by a male's morbid, obsessive fear that his penis is shrinking and being reabsorbed, or by a female's morbid, obsessive belief that her breasts and labia are shrinking and being sucked inside her body. It is associated with a belief that ghosts have no genitals, and that the skrinkage of the penis implies impending death. The disorder occurs principally in southern

China, Malaysia, and Borneo, and may be linked with guilt associated with masturbation and "promiscuity." The persons affected by the fears often will call on family members and friends for help in preventing the dreaded genital reabsorption. Derived from Malay. The male form of the disorder is sometimes called **shook yong**, which means "shrinking penis" in Chinese.

*If Tom had not possessed an extremely small phallus, he would probably not have been susceptible to **koro** during his two-year visit to Malaysia.*

korophilia (kor-o-FIL-ē-ə): the tendency to fall in love with a male younger than oneself, including a woman's preference for extremely young men. Derived from Greek *koros* (boy, lad) and *philia* (attachment, attraction).

*Because she was a wealthy and beautiful middle-aged woman who looked younger than she was, Barbara could easily indulge her **korophilia**.*

kystapaza (kī-stə-PAZ/PÄZ-ə): a vagina giving the sensation of snatching or snapping the male organ. Derived from Greek *kysthos* (vagina) and *harpazein* (to snap up).

*Clark appreciated Lois's enthusiasm, exuberant sexuality, and her fit body, including her **kystapaza**.*

L

lactaphilia (*lak*-tə-FIL-ē-ə): sexual arousal from lactating breasts. Derived from Latin *lac, lact-* (milk) and Greek *philia* (attachment, attraction).

*There are many reasons for **lactaphilia**, including the development of a conditioned response from people's having been breast fed as infants.*

lagnatrophy (lag-NAT-rə-fē): partial or total disappearance of sexual craving, as in old age. Derived from Greek *lagneia* (lust) and *atrophos* (ill fed).

*There are many physically robust men who never experience **lagnatrophy**, even in old age.*

lagnechia (lag-NEK-ē-ə): a feeling of incomplete satisfaction after orgasm, as when one's tension is not fully relieved. Derived from Greek *lagneia* (lust) and *echo* (to hold, restrain).

*Dash felt frustrated, and could not understand his **lagnechia** after having unrestrained sex with Elly.*

lagnekinetic (lag-nə-ki-NET-ic): pertaining to sexually arousing movement of a body, especially a female one. Derived from Greek *lagneia* (lust) and *kinesis* (movement).

In the movie Striptease, *Demi Moore performed **lagnekinetic** dances.*

lagnephronesis (lag-nə-frō-NĒ-sis): preoccupation with lustful thoughts. Derived from Greek *lagneia* (lust) and *kinesis* (movement).

*Since the Roman Catholic Church teaches that "impure thoughts" are sinful, it condemns **lagnephronesis**.*

lagnesis (lag-NĒ-sis): excessively strong sexual desire. Derived from Greek *lagneia* (lust).

*When Stan told Eric that Eric's gonorrhea was due proximately to bacteria but remotely to **lagnesis**, Eric had no idea what Stan was talking about.*

lagnocolysis (*lag*-nə-kə-LĪ-sis): inhibition of sexual desire. Derived from Greek *lagneia* (lust) and *kolysis* (hindrance, impediment).

*Since many narcissistic politicians nearly always think about sex, they could probably profit from **lagnocolysis**.*

lagnocopia (lag-nə-KŌP-ē-ə): a weariness from sexual debauchery. Derived from Greek *lagneia* (lust) and *kopos* (weariness).

*We asked the energetic porn star how he could perform sexually almost constantly without experiencing **lagnocopia**.*

lagnodomnia (lag-nə-DOM-nē-ə): a man's ability to delay his orgasm to prolong intercourse, enabling his female partner to experience and enjoy her orgasm. Derived from Greek *lagneia* (lust) and Latin *dominari* (to rule).

*Jane complimented Jethro on his **lagnodomnia**, which enabled her to have sufficient stimulation to climax.*

lagnofugia (lagnə-FŌŌ-jē-ə): avoidance, conscious or unconscious, of any thoughts or activities dealing in any way with sex. Derived from Greek *lagneia* (lust) and Latin *fugere* (to flee).

*We were not sure whether her **lagnofugia** was a product of her religious upbringing, or a fear that she would not be able to avoid sex once her desires were piqued.*

lagnoia (lag-NOI-ə): a sexually obsessed state of mind. Derived from Greek *lagneia* (lust) and *nous* (mind).

*The mother lamented that many advertisements for teens, much popular music, and many TV shows and movies inspire or at least deepen **lagnoia** instead of turning people's minds to nonsexual matters.*

lagnolalia (lag-nə-LĀL-ē-ə): obscene language, especially when habitual. Derived from Greek *lagneia* (lust) and *lalia* (talk, conversation).

*Anyone who has listened to the language in an Eddie Murphy comedy routine knows that he enjoys using **lagnolalia**.*

lagnopathic (lag-nə/nō-PATH-ik): pathologically lustful. Derived from Greek *lagneia* (lust) and *pathos* (emotion, passion, suffering).

*Our sexology teacher told us that, if the basketball player Wilt Chamberlain really did sleep with thousands of women, he was almost certainly **lagnopathic**.*

lagnopathy (lag-NOP-ə-thē): pathological lust. Derived from Greek *lagneia* (lust) and *pathos* (emotion, passion, suffering).

*Many people would argue that a person can be affected by **lagnopathy**, and still be an outstanding public servant.*

lagnoperissia (lag-nə-pur-RIZ-ē-e): the condition of having too much lust. Derived from Greek *lagneia* (lust) and *perisseia* (abundance, surplus).

*The psychiatrist insisted that his patient's suffered from **lagnoperissia**, since indulging his libido interfered with the ability to earn a living and to discharge his other responsibilities.*

lagnoprivous (lag-nə-PRI/PRĪ-vəs): lacking sexual interest, as a person, movie, book, and so on. Derived from Greek *lagneia* (lust) and Latin *privare* (to deprive).

Although Bob Guccione's movie Caligula *was advertised as sexy, it was largely **lagnoprivous**, short on sex and long on violence.*

lagnoserotinous (lag-nə-se-ROT-i-nus): attaining full sexual vigor late in life, especially in men. Derived from Greek *lagneia* (lust) and Latin *serotinus* (ripe late in the season or life).

*Many **lagnoserotinous** men are people who took years overcoming negative ideas they acquired about sex early in life.*

lapactor (lə-PAK-tor): the male sex organ, especially when erect. Derived from Greek *lapassein* (to discharge).

*The elderly female former porn star asserted that a man's intelligence is sexier to her than any **lapactor**.*

lascive (lə-SĒV): lustful; **lascivious** (*see entry*). Derived from Latin *lascivus* (wanton).

*TV soup stars often portray **lascive** people who are usually having sex with persons to whom they are not married.*

lascivia (lə-SIV-ē-ə): intense sexual desire; lust. Derived from Latin *lascivus* (wanton).

In literature and mythology, the goat has been a symbol of **lascivia**.

lascivious (lə-SIV-ē-əs): inclined to lechery; lewd; lustful; tending to arouse sexual desire, as in "lascivious verse." Derived from Latin *lascivus* (wanton).

The Democrat senator asserted that Republicans were more interested in Bill Clinton's **lascivious** *practices than in completing America's business.*

lascivious cohabitation (lə-SIV-ē-əs kō-hab-i-TĀ-shən): an old, usually legal, term for living together with "sexual privileges," with or without marriage.

The minister lamented that his unmarried daughter is living in **lascivious cohabitation**.

lavacultophilia (lə-va-kul-tə-FIL-ē-ə): a proclivity for watching females in bathing suits. Derived from Latin *lavatio* (bathing), Latin *cultus* (suit, attire), and Greek *philia* (attachment, attraction).

The famous swimsuit issue of Sports Illustrated *appeals to not only those with* **lavacultophilia** *but also to people who enjoy looking at beautiful women in erotic poses.*

lécheur (lesh-UR): a man who performs oral sex on a woman. Derived from Old French *lechier* (to lick) and a masculine suffix.

The satirical magazine National Lampoon *once featured a spread on "wife tasting," in which blindfolded* **lécheurs** *were to identify their wives.*

lécheuse (lay-Sə(R)Z): a woman who performs oral sex on a man. Derived from Old French *lechier* (to lick) and a feminine suffix.

The **lécheuse** *would suck on some strong mints immediately before oral sex to give her husband additional stimulation.*

lectamia (lek-TAM/TĀM-ē-ə): caressing and other amorous contact in bed without coitus. Derived from Latin *lectus* (bed) and *amor* (love).

Since Claudia enjoyed caressing, but did not want to risk pregnancy, she and Lyndon would restrict their sex play to **lectamia**.

lectual (LEK-chōō-əl): suitable for the bed; also can mean "bedridden." Derived from Latin *lectus* (bed).

Greg would sometimes relate his **lectual** *pleasures to his two sons.*

lectualia (*lek*-chōō-Ā-lē-ə): sexual orgies accompanied by drinking. Derived from Latin *lectus* (a bed).

Some Romans participated in **lectualia** *in which all or almost all conceivable sexual acts were permitted.*

lectulate (LEK-chōō-lāt): to spend much time in bed, especially in sexual pursuits. Derived from Latin *lectus* (a bed).

Mary warned her son that, if he ever decides to **lectulate** *in their home, she will think about taking away his allowance.*

legorastia (leg-ə-RAS-tē-ə): the tendency to be aroused from watching a woman's lips while she speaks. Derived from Latin *lego* (to speak, recite) and Greek *erastes* (lover).

Milton, a speech pathologist, had trouble helping his clients because his **legorastia** *would distract him from concentrating on their problems.*

leptosadism (lep-tō-SĀ-dizəm): a mild form of sadism, including mild humiliation and spanking in a sexual context. Derived from Greek *leptos* (fine, thin, delicate) and *sadism* (from the cruel sexual practices of Comte Donaten Alphonse Francois [Marquis] de Sade [1740–1814]).

Millard and Abigail enjoyed gently spanking each other, and engaged in other forms of **leptosadism***.*

lesbophobia (lez-bə/bō-FŌB-ē-ə): the fear of lesbians. Derived from the name of the island of Lesbos (now Mytilene) and its connection with the reputed lesbian band associated with the ancient female poet Sappho.

In the current U.S. military, open expressions of lesbianism are outlawed and so are open expressions of **lesbophobia***.*

libertine (LIB-ur-tēn): a person, usually a man, who is unrestrained in sexual indulgence. Derived from Latin *libertinus* (of freedmen).

The great basketball player Wilt Chamberlain was a **libertine** *who bragged about having slept with thousands of women.*

libidacoria (li-bid-ə-KOR-ē-ə): a sexual craving incapable of being satisfied. Derived from Latin *libido* (sexual desire), Greek *a-* (without), and Greek *koros* (satiety).

We felt sorry for Jimmy because of his **libidacoria***, which his countless sexual trysts never satisfied.*

libidocenosis (li-bi-dō-se-NŌ-sis, li-bē-dō-se-NŌ-sis): the removal or release of sexual tension by sexual indulgence. Derived from Latin *libido* (lust, sex drive) and Greek *kenosis* (an emptying).

Right before his **libidocenosis***, the playboy would quote the poet William Blake, who wrote, "The road to excess leads to the palace of wisdom."*

libidocratia (li-*bidō*-KRAT-ē-ə): the condition in which people's libido is the focal point of their being and lives. Derived from Latin *libido* (desire, lust) and Greek *kratos* (power).

*When people organize all their efforts and time around having sex, they have given themselves over to **libidocratia**.*

libidolambosis (li-bi-dō-lam-BŌ-sis, li-*bē*-dō-lam-BŌ-sis): the awakening of sexual desire by licking, as someone's sexual organs. Derived from Latin *libido* and *lambo* (to lick).

*When Alice said that her difficulties with Sam were licked, we had no idea that she was alluding to **libidolambosis**.*

libidoneurosis (li-bid-ō-nōō-RŌ-sis, li-bē-dō-nōō-RŌ-sis): neurotic frustration due to the failure to satisfy one's sexual desires. Derived from Latin *libido* (desire, lust) and Greek *neur-* (nerve) and *-osis* (condition).

*George became so frustrated because of Jane's unwillingness to continue to have relations with him that he developed **libidoneurosis**.*

libidopath (li-BID-ō-path): a person with cravings so unusual or intense as to qualify as "abnormal." Derived from Latin *libido* (lust, desire) and Greek *pathos* (passion, emotion, suffering).

Woody Allen's movie Everything You Always Wanted to Know About Sex (But Were Afraid to Ask) *contained depictions of some **libidopaths**, including a man who became sexually and emotionally attached to a sheep, and a couple who felt impelled to have sex as often as possible in public places.*

libidopause (li-bi-dō-PÔZ, li-*bē*-dō-pôz): the time in people's lives when their libido begins to decline. Derived from Latin *libido* (lust, sex drive) and *pausa* (a stopping).

*The well-dressed elderly man told the young streetwalker that she needs to find men who are not experiencing **libidopause**.*

libidosyntonia (li-bi-dō-sin-TŌN-ē-ə, li-bē-dō-sin-TŌN-ē-ə): the state of sexual responsiveness to the demands of married life. Derived from Latin *libido* (lust, sex drive) and Greek *syntonos* (being in harmony with).

*The marriage counselor held that **libidosyntonia** is often most important the first year or two of marriage, when satisfying sex can help a newly married couple withstand marital stress.*

lubricious (lōō-BRISH-es): wanton; lecherous. Derived from the Latin *lubricus* (slippery).

*The **lubricious** young man boasted that he is so horny that the crack of dawn had better watch out.*

lupae (LOO -pī): an obsolete term for "prostitutes." Derived from Latin *lupa* (female wolf) because of the custom of prostitutes in ancient Rome of attracting customers with wolf calls.

*Many men vacation in Costa Rica just for the **lupae**, some of whom are adolescents.*

lupanar (loo-PĀ-nər): a whorehouse; brothel. Derived from Latin *lupa* (prostitute, "she-wolf").

*Some married men go to **lupanars** for oral sex and other practices that they cannot get at home.*

lygerastia (lī-jur-RAS-tē-ə): the tendency to become romantic or erotic in a darkened or partly darkened room. Derived from Greek *lyge* (twilight) and *erastes* (lover).

*Because Jeannie was used to living in dark surroundings and felt most romantic in darkened rooms, her boyfriend Tony put aluminum foil on his windows to stimulate her **lygerastia**.*

lygerevirescence (lī-jur-*rev*-ir-ES-əns): a renewal of interest in lovemaking late in life, especially in women. Derived from Greek *lyge* (twilight) and Latin *revirescence* (a renewal, a growing young again).

*Abraham said that the birth of his son was due in part to Sarah's **lygerevirescence**.*

M

machlobasia (mak-lō-BĀ-zhə): pleasurable sensation experienced by some women, especially obese ones, during walking, when the thighs rub against the labia. Derived from Greek *machlos* (lustful) and Latin *basis* (base).

*We were not sure whether the heavyset woman walking away from us was smiling because of **machlobasia** or some other reason.*

macrogenitalism (mak-rō-JEN-i-tl-izəm): arousal from large genitals. Derived from Greek *makros* (long), Latin *gignere* (to beget), and *-ism*.

*The well-endowed porn star John Holmes appealed to those with a taste for **macrogenitalism**.*

macromastia (mak-rō-MAS-tē-ə): a condition of having unusually large breasts, often associated with hypertrophied milk ducts and an abnormal increase in fat and fibrous connective tissue. Derived from Greek *makros* (long) and *mastos* (breast).

*People would rarely notice Sheila's face, since her **macromastia** attracted attention to her breasts.*

macrophallia (mak-rō-FAL-lē-ə): the condition of having an unusually large penis. Derived from Greek *macros* (long) and *phallos* (penis).

*Dick was so embarrassed by his **macrophallia** that he would wear baggy pants.*

macrophallus (mak-rō-FAL-ləs): an extraordinarily large penis. Derived from Greek *makros* (long) and *phallos* (penis).

*Because of Forrest's **macrophallus**, people used to tease him, suggesting that he could lie on his back and hit low-flying seagulls.*

madefaction (*mad*-ə-FAK-shən): the process of a woman's becoming "wet," or having her genitalia oiled or lubricated by natural secretions, as when she is sexually aroused. Derived from Latin *madefacere* (to make wet).

*The mere sight of certain men, including Tom Cruise, Brad Pitt, and Richard Gere, is enough to excite **madefaction** in countless women.*

maieusiophilia (mā-ū-zē-ō-FIL-ē-ə): arousal from pregnant women. Derived from Greek *maieutikos* (of midwifery) and *philia* (attachment, attraction).

*Buford's **maieusiophilia** led him to work at a maternity shop and to buy magazines such as* Milky Mamas.

maieusiophobia (mā-ū-zē-ō-FŌB-ē-ə): an intense and morbid fear of childbirth. Derived from Greek *maieusthai* (to act as a midwife), and *phobos* (fear).

*Some advocates of natural childbirth believe that **maieusiophobia** often plays a role in causing difficult labor.*

malaxomania (mə-laks-ō-MĀN-ē-ə): a strong craving to "knead" the flesh of a woman, especially the breasts. Derived from Greek *malaxatio* (act of softening).

*Eve would sometimes have bruised breasts because of Adam's exuberant **malaxomania**.*

malaxophilia (mə-laks-ō-FIL-ē-ə): a male's fondness for "kneading" a woman's flesh, especially the breasts. Derived from Greek *malaxatio* (act of softening) and *philia* (attachment, attraction).

Jason's teacher warned him against indulging his **malaxophilia** *with Medea in the school cafeteria.*

malaxophobia (mə-laks-ō-FŌB-ē-ə): a woman's fear of having her flesh, especially breasts, "kneaded" by a man. Derived from Greek *malaxatio* (act of softening) and Greek *phobos* (fear).

Beatrice told Dante that she was not suffering from **malaxophobia** *but simply had sensitive breasts, which cause her discomfort when they are manhandled.*

malleation (môl/mal-lē-Ā-shən): a series of rapid, hammerlike thrusts made by the male sex organ during intercourse, often expressing an enthusiasm and eagerness, as after a long period of abstinence. Derived from Latin *malleare* (to hammer).

Jane's vulgar sister told her that anyone who gets nailed by a sex-hungry carpenter should expect **malleation**.

mamilla (mə-MIL-ə): nipple. Derived from the Latin diminutive of *mamma* (breast).

While some dress codes are relaxed enough to allow women to display part of their breasts, few dress codes will allow a woman to display a **mamilla**.

mammalingus (*mam-ə-LING-gəs*): oral sex performed on the female breast. Derived from Latin *mamma* (breast) and *lingere* (to lick).

When Theodore asserted that nursing is usually highly beneficial for babies, Eddie, who was fond of **mammalingus**, *responded that it is also good for adults.*

mammaquatia (*mam-ə-KWAT-ē-ə*): the bobbing or the oscillation of a woman's breasts, as during dancing, running, or exercising. Derived from Latin *mamma* (breast) and *quatio* (to shake).

According to a television executive, the old TV show Battle of the Network Stars *was about athletic prowess, not* **mammaquatia**.

mammaskepsis (*mam-ə-SKEP-sis*): the ogling of women's breasts or their contours. Derived from Latin *mamma* (breast) and Greek *skopein* (to observe).

Dolly Parton has been used to being on the receiving end of **mammaskepsis**.

mammose (mam-MŌS): having large breasts. Derived from Latin *mamma* (breast) and *-ose* (full of).

*Although **mammose** women attract many men and intimidate or repel others, they are nearly always noticed.*

manevalent (man-ə-VĀL-ənt): sexually potent only in the morning, as when some older men have erections only upon awakening with a full bladder. Derived from Latin *mane* (the early morning) and *valero* (to be strong).
*Unless the **manevalent** man had intercourse soon after awaking in the morning, he would not be able to have it later in the day.*

manipulus (mə-NIP-ū-ləs): a handful of female flesh, such as what is seized by a man's hand during lovemaking. Derived from Latin *manus* (hand) and Greek *pleres* (full).
*Edith warned Archie against being excessively rough when treating her right breast as a **manipulus**.*

manotripsis (man-ō-TRIP-sis): the act of masturbating a man. Derived from Latin *manus* (hand) and Greek *tribein* (to rub).
In the movie Animal House *a college co-ed was performing **manotripsis** while wearing a glove.*

manuxorate (mə-NÔKS-ə-rāt): of a male, to masturbate; literally, "to make one's hand a wife." Derived from Latin *manus* (hand) and *uxor* (wife).
In the movie Love and Death, *Woody Allen alluded to his propensity to **manuxorate** when he said that he had learned to make love through a great of practice—while alone.*

maritate (*mer*-i-TĀT): to manipulate one's vulva by hand; of females, to masturbate. Derived from Latin *maritus* (husband), with the suggestion that one's hand is acting as a husband. (*See* **manuxorate**.)
*Rosie asserted that when her husband goes on a six-month cruise for the navy, she **maritates**, satisfying her libido while protecting her marriage from temptations and herself from sexually transmissible diseases.*

martymachlia (mär-tē-MAK-lē-ə): a settled desire to require the presence of several other persons as observers during one's lovemaking, a form of exhibitionism. Derived from Greek *martys* (witness) and *machlos* (lustful).
*The client with **martymachlia** demanded that he and his prostitute be moved from their private room to the "grope room" so that he would have spectators.*

maschalingus (mas-kəl-LING-gəs): licking of someone's armpit. Derived from Greek *maschale* (armpit) and Latin *lingere* (to lick).

*Ulysses asked Julia to avoid underarm deodorants the days he plans to perform **maschalingus**, since he likes the natural taste of an armpit.*

maschalolagnia (mas-kəl-lō/lə-LAG-nē-ə): sexual arousal from viewing an exposed female armpit. Derived from Greek *maschale* (armpit) and *lagneia* (lust).
   *His **maschalolagnia** was stimulated by seeing female tennis players serve.*

maschalophallation (mas-kəl-lō/lə-FAL-la-shən): male penetration of the female armpit. Derived from Greek *maschale* (armpit) and *phallos* (penis).
   *Sarah liked wearing sleeveless clothes so that she and her boyfriend could enjoy some quick **maschalophallation**.*

maschalophilemia (mas-kəl-*lō*-fi-LĒ-mē-ə): erotic kissing of the female armpit. Derived from Greek *maschale* (armpit) and *philema* (a kiss).
   *Desmond enjoyed **maschalophilemia**, but only after his girlfriend had shaved her armpits.*

maschalophilous (mas-kəl-LOF-ə-ləs): especially attracted to armpits. Derived from Greek *maschale* (armpit) and *philein* (to love).
   *We did not realize that Bertrand was **maschalophilous** until we saw him offering to pay women to shave their armpits.*

mastigophoric (mas-ti-gə-FOR-ik): pertaining to carrying a whip. Derived from the Greek *mastig(o)-* (whip), from *mastix* (whip), and *pherein* (to carry). The word literally refers to a class of Protozoa whose members have flagella or whiplike structures.
   *We were surprised that the shy woman had a poster of Madonna in one of the star's **mastigophoric** poses.*

mastigothymia (mas-ti-gō-THĪ-mē-ə): erotic pleasure from real or imaginary whipping; also sexual pleasure aroused in a person because of being whipped. Derived from Greek *mastig(o)-* (whip), from *mastix* (whip), and *epithymia* (lust).
   *Flavia assured us that the marks on her back were not from abuse, but from rough sex games, including **mastigothymia**.*

mastilagnia (mas-ti-LAG-nē-ə): sexual gratification from being whipped; the urge to be whipped for sexual gratification. Derived from Greek *mastig(o)-* (whip), from *mastix*, whip, and *lagneia* (lust).
   *Although—or perhaps because—Robert was a powerful executive during the day, he would enjoy being treated roughly by female bodybuilders at night, even to the point of indulging his **mastilagnia**.*

mastolator (mas-tō/tə-LĀT-or): a man who worships female breasts. Derived from Greek *mastos* (breast) and *latreia* (worship).

In the 1963 movie It's A Mad Mad Mad Mad World, *comic actor Terry Thomas, a Britisher, suggests that all American men are* **mastolators**, *with an insatiable attraction to female breasts.*

mastophallation (mas-tō/tə-FAL-lā-shən): the act of moving one's penis back and forth between two female breasts; intermammary intercourse. Derived from Greek *mastos* (breast) and *phallos* (penis).

When Greg saw the large, shapely breasts of his son's girlfriend, he reminded Jeremiah that **mastophallation** *is safe sex.*

mastophrenia (mas-tə-FRĒN-ē-ə): obsessive thinking about female breasts. Derived from Greek *mastos* (breast) and *phren* (mind, diaphragm).

Our principal told our class that, because young males do not need incitement to **mastophrenia**, *any girl who arrives at school without a bra will be sent home.*

mastunculi (mas-TUNGK-ū-lī): small, underdeveloped breasts. Derived from Greek *mastos* (breast) and Latin *-unculus* (diminutive suffix).

Because of the current obsession with thinness, many female celebrities who would have been criticized years ago for possessing **mastunculi** *are now often considered fashionably slender.*

masturbism (MAS-tur-bizəm): chronic masturbation. Derived from Latin *masturbari* [perhaps from *manus* (hand) and *stuprare* (to defile, deflower)].

Algernon wondered whether spending eight hours every day masturbating constitutes **masturbism**.

masturbosis (mas-tur-BŌ-sis): "mental disorder" from the mental conflict attendant on some people's masturbation. Derived from Latin *masturbari* [perhaps from *manus* (hand) and *stuprare* (to defile, deflower)] and *-osis* (condition).

The sexologist told us that masturbation alone need not cause any mental problems at all, but when masturbators regard masturbation as extremely sinful, they can experience **masturbosis**.

matrolagnia (matrō-LAG-nē-ə): sexual love of a son for his mother. Derived from Latin *mater* (mother) and Greek *lagneia* (lust).

The character portrayed by actor Lawrence Harvey in The Manchurian Candidate *had an unusual relationship with his mother, possibly involving* **matrolagnia**.

matronolagnia (matronō-LAG-nē-ə): sexual attraction to older women. Derived from Latin *matrona* (matron, woman of rank) and Greek *lagneia* (lust).

When Brian, who was twenty, seemed to be romantically interested in his best friend's grandmother, we began to recognize his **matronolagnia**.

matutolagnia (mə-*tōōt*-ə-LAG-nē-ə): lust in the morning. Derived from Latin *matutinus* (of the morning, early in the morning) and Greek *lagneia* (lust).

When we asked Victor whether he exercised in the morning, he replied that he gets enough exercise simply by indulging his **matutolagnia**.

matutorthosis (mə/ma-tōō-tor-THŌ-sis): a morning erection, usually because of a full bladder. Derived from Latin *matutinus* (of the morning, early in the morning), Greek *orthos* (straight, right, true), and Greek *-osis* (action, process, condition).

When Eileen saw Greg's **matutorthosis**, *she told him that he needed to use it or lose it.*

mazauxesis (mə/ma-zôk-ZĒ-sis): overdevelopment of female breasts. Derived from Greek *mazos, mastos* (breast) and *auxesis* (increase, growth).

Many women with **mazauxesis** *choose to get breast reduction surgery.*

mazectenia (ma/mə-zek-TĒN-ē-ə): a condition defined by hanging breasts. Derived from Greek *mazos, mastos* (breast) and *ekteino* (to prolong).

Because of Dolly's **mazectenia**, *she would walk with a stoop.*

mazmassation (maz-mas-SĀ-shən): the kneading of female breasts. Derived from Greek *mazos, mastos* (breast) and *massein* (to knead).

When the young man said that hands and breasts go as well together as ham and eggs, we suspected that he practiced **mazmassation**.

mazocentric (māzō/mazo-SEN-trik): pertaining to the centering of male libido on female breasts. Derived from *mazos, mastos* (breast) and Greek *kentron* (center of a circle).

Our commander told us that he will not tolerate **mazocentric** *ogling, especially among enlisted men.*

mazorhicnosis (māzə-rik-NŌ-sis, māzər-rik-NŌ-sis): the shriveling of female breasts with age. Derived from Greek *mazos, mastos* (breast) and *rhiknosis* (a shriveling).

When Dwight looked at Mamie's breasts and commented negatively on her **mazorhicnosis**, *she replied, "What do you expect? I am 105."*

mazotropism (māz-ō-TRŌP-izəm, māze-TRŌP-izəm): the tendency of female breasts to affect and attract males. Derived from the Greek *mazos* (breast) and *trepein* (to turn).

*Although Freud spoke of penis envy, he might have spoken, with even more plausibility, of breast envy, given the obvious fact of **mazotropism**.*

meable (MĒ-əbl): easily penetrated. Derived from Latin *meatus* (passage, opening).

*The drunken scholar told the prostitute that he would enjoy penetrating all her **meable** orifices.*

meatosthesia (mē-at-ə-*STHĒ*-zhə): the condition of having erotic sensitivity in every bodily opening, such as the mouth, anus, and vagina. Derived from Latin *meatus* (passage, opening) and Greek *aisthesis* (feeling or sensitivity).

*Because of Jen's **meatosthesia**, she told her husband to treat her every orifice as a playground.*

meatus (mē-Ā-təs): a small opening or passageway to a body organ. Derived from Latin for "passage," from *meare* (to go).

*Because we did not want to offend the rude man, we did not call him an asshole, but rather an anal **meatus**.*

medectasia (me-dek-TĀZHə): the bulging of an erect penis, as in the front of one's pants. Derived from Greek *medos* (penis) and *ekstasis* (state of being beside oneself, a protruding).

When former Vice President Albert Gore posed on the cover of Rolling Stone Magazine, *the cover appeared to depict **medectasia**, or someone with a large sock in his pants.*

medectophobia (me-dek-tə-FŌB-ē-ə): a male's fear that the contour of his penis will be discernible, as because of an erection in tight pants. Derived from Greek *medos* (penis), *ekstasis* (state of being beside oneself, a protruding), and *phobos* (fear).

*His **medectophobia** was so severe that it prompted the adolescent to wear pants that would have engulfed King Kong.*

mederigentic (med-eri-JEN-tik): stimulating (in males) the desire for sexual intercourse. Derived from Greek *medos* (penis) and *erigentic* (exciting, stimulating).

*For many men, pornography can be **mederigentic**.*

medisect (MED-ə-sekt): the cleft between a woman's breasts. Derived from Latin *medius* (middle) and *secare* (to cut).

> *Ridgely enjoyed watching the woman in her bikini because he was able to get a good view of her **medisect**.*

medochnoia (med-ok/ək-NOI-ə): the condition of having a male organ that is gentle rather than harsh to women during lovemaking. Derived from Greek *medos* (penis) and *chnous* (any light, porous substance, foam, fine down, bloom).

> *The prostitute complimented the gentle client on his **medochnoia**.*

medocurix (med-ō-KŪ-riks, med-ō-KUR-iks): a woman who practices cosmetic care of the male sex organ and the genital area, as by applying cream to the skin, clipping pubic hair, or massaging the genitals. Women have performed this cosmetological specialty since ancient times, when slave girls and concubines applied fragrant lotions to the sex organs of their masters. Derived from Greek *medos* (penis) and Latin *cura* (care).

> *The talented **medocurix** asserted that she was there for cosmetic care only and had no suctorial duties.*

medolalia (med-ō-LĀL-ē-ə): obscene language about the penis. (*See* **phallolalia**.) Derived from Greek *medos* (penis) and *lalia* (conversation, chatter).

> *When the minister overheard his congregants' **medolalia**, he told them that they were in a church, not a brothel.*

medomalacophobia (med-ō-mal-ak-ə-FŌB-ē-ə): the fear, mostly of men, that the erected sex organ will become flaccid during intercourse. Not surprisingly, the fear itself can become a self-fulfilling prophecy, since psychology can influence physiology. Derived from Greek *medos* (penis), Latin *malaxo* (to soften), and Greek *phobos* (fear).

> *Raymond's preoccupation with his sexual technique led him to suffer from **medomalacophobia**, which in turn caused his phallus to become soft under stress.*

melissophilia (me/mə-lissə/lissō-FIL-ē-ə): attraction to, or arousal from, bees or bee stings. Some men will capture bees to use them to sting the glans penis (head) to extend the duration of an orgasm, to increase the circumference of the penis, and to enhance the sensations felt in the penis. Derived from Greek *melissa* (honey bee) and *philia* (attachment, attraction).

> *When the physician saw the enlarged head of the penis, bearing what*

looked like two bee stings, he asked the adolescent whether he was given to **melissophilia.**

melolagnia (melō-LAG-nē-ə): sexual desire aroused by music. Derived from Greek *melos* (song) and *lagneia* (lust).
   Early condemnations of rock music were motivated to some degree by a fear of a sexual anarchy induced by **melolagnia.**

mentulhedonia (men-chōōl-hē-DŌN-ē-ə): pride or satisfaction from being a man or having a male sex organ. Derived from Latin *mentula* (penis) and Greek *hedone* (pleasure).
   The feminist asserted that men who understandably have little confidence in their intelligence will often take refuge in **mentulhedonia.**

mentulomania (men-chōōl-ə-MĀN-ē-ə): masturbation or any obsessive thought or compulsive action concerning one's penis. Derived from Latin *mentula* (penis) and Greek *mania* (madness, craving).
   When Woody Allen called his brain his "second favorite organ" in one of his movies, he might have revealed **mentulomania.**

mentulophrenia (men-chōōl-ə/ō-FRĒN-ē-ə): obsessive thoughts of the penis. Derived from Latin *mentula* (penis) and Greek *phren* (mind, diaphragm).
   When Alfred accused Sigmund of **mentulophrenia**, *Sigmund responded, "Are you kidding? It wasn't I who put phallic symbols everywhere!"*

mentulophreniac (men-chōōl-ə-FRĒN-ē-ak): a nymphomanic persistently thinking of penises. Derived from Latin *mentula* (penis) and Greek *phren* (mind, diaphragm).
   While many men like to think that **mentulophreniacs** *await them on every corner, most women are not obsessed with the male organ.*

meretrix (MER-ə-triks): an obsolete Latin term for "prostitute." Derived from Latin *mereo* ("I earn").
   The **meretrix** *boasted that she is a member of a profession that is a great boost to motels.*

merintholagnia (mer-in-thō-LAG-nē-ə): masochism in which subjects achieve sexual pleasure from being immobilized by a rope. Derived from Greek *merinthos* (cord) and *lagneia* (lust).
   Because David enjoyed making puns and indulging his **merintholagnia**, *he would tell people on his telephone answering machine that, when he doesn't answer the phone, he is all tied up.*

merkin (MUR-kin): a woman's pubic wig, often either replacing missing hairs or covering hair of one color with hair of another color. To appear more attractive, some prostitutes will wear merkins of uncommon colors, as when they wear blonde ones in a country of mostly dark-haired people. Although the origin of "merkin" is unknown, we do know that the term from the sixteenth to the eighteenth century used to refer to a woman's natural pubic hair and even to her genitalia. Incidentally, the word occurs in plural on someone's shirt in the 1994 movie "PCU" (for "Politically Correct University"). The word was also the name of a Peter Sellers character in *Dr. Strangelove*.

*When the man told his wife that she had the most attractive **merkin** in town, she asked him how he knew.*

merophilous (me/mə-ROF-i-ləs): especially attracted to female thighs. Derived from Greek *meros* (thigh) and *philein* (to love).

*While the exercise instructor encouraged women to wear extremely short shorts ostensibly to give them freer movement, we knew about his **merophilous** motives.*

merphallation (mer-FAL-lā-shən): intercourse between someone's thighs; interfemoral intercourse. Derived from Greek *meros* (thigh) and *phallos* (penis).

*Because Zachary was fond of Margaret's thighs and wanted to engage in safe sex, he suggested **merphallation**.*

misogamist (mi-SOG-ə-mist): one who hates marriage. Derived from Greek *misein* (to hate)/*misos* (hatred) and *gamos* (marriage).

*The **misogamist** said that marriage is a fine institution, but that he did not want to live in an institution.*

misogynist (mi-SOJ-ə-nist): one who hates women. Derived from Greek *misein* (to hate)/*misos* (hatred) and *gune, gyn-* (woman).

*The German philosopher Schopenhauer was a **misogynist** who believed that women are less intelligent than men.*

misophileist (mis-ō-FIL-ē-ist): one who dislikes kissing or being kissed. Derived from Greek *misein* (to hate) and *philema* (a kiss).

*The lips of the **misophileist** were untouched by other lips because of his fear of germs.*

mixoscopia (miks-ə-SKŌ-pē-ə, miks-ə-SKO-pē-ə): sexual gratification from watching others have sex. Derived from Greek *mixis* (a mingling) and *skopein* (to observe).

*Given the millions of persons who enjoy pornography, the desires involved
in* **mixoscopia** *are doubtless common.*

mixoscopic zoophilia (miks-ə-SKO-pik zōe-FIL-ē-ə): sexual arousal from
watching animals have sex. Derived from the Greek *mixis* [a mingling, as in
apomixis (asexual reproduction)], *skopein* (to observe), *zoon* (animal), and
philia (attachment, attraction). The expression is used and defined in
Havelock Ellis's *Studies in the Psychology of Sex.*
   We did not realize that Gordon was affected by **mixoscopic zoophilia**
until we saw him masturbating while watching the two horses mate.

monopedomania (mono-ped-ə-MĀN-ē-ə): arousal from intercourse with
one-legged partners, usually women. The French author Montaigne wrote
in the sixteenth century: "It is a common proverb in Italy that anyone who
has not lain with a limping woman does not know the perfect pleasure of
Venus" (*Essays*, III, xi).
   There is a bedroom scene with a one-legged woman in the movie Deuce
Bigelow, Male Gigolo *that may appeal to viewers with*
monopedomania*.*

morphophilia (mor-fō-FIL-ē-ə): attraction to, or arousal from, a person
with a different physique from one's own. Derived from Greek *morphe*
(form) and *philia* (attachment, attraction).
   The short, petite woman revealed her **morphophilia** *by her dating only
tall and husky football players.*

mort douce (môr dōos): French for "sweet death," referring either to death
during intercourse ("death in the saddle"), or to the bliss following orgasm.
   Men who have weak hearts are more likely to suffer **mort douce** *when
they are having intercourse with paramours than with their wives.*

mucophagy (mū-KOF-ə-je): the consumption of nasal mucosa, usually
done as a matter of course in **nasolingus** (*see entry*). Some people like
mucophagy because of the novelty of it, others because of a desire for
degradation, and still others because of a desire to demonstrate complete
acceptance and love of their partners. Derived from Latin *mucus* (slime,
mucus) and Greek *phagein* (to eat).
   *When Boris discovered that Natasha had a stuffed nose because of her
allergies, he knew that his appetite for* **mucophagy** *would soon be
satisfied by an all-you-can-eat nasal feast.*

mulcage (MUL-kəj, MUL-käzh): the satisfaction or appeasement of an
erection by stroking, especially with a female hand. Derived from Latin

mulceo (to stroke, soften, soothe), and *-age* (suffix designating states, conditions, or results).
*After Sabrina's helping satisfy Darrin by engaging in **mulcage**, Darrin thanked her for that small kindness.*

muliebration (mū-lē-e-BRĀ-shən): the assumption of female characteristics by males. Derived from Latin *mulier* (woman).
*Men who have strong feelings about gender roles often become upset at **muliebration**.*

muliebria (mū-lē-EBRĒə): female sex organs. Derived from Latin *mulier* (woman).
*When it was quite clear that the sex scandal had destroyed Randy's political career, he told his constituents that he was not so provincial as to appreciate the **muliebria** of only his wife but was capable of loving all **muliebria**.*

muliebrity (mū-lē-EB-ri-tē): the state of being a woman; womanhood; womanliness; femininity. Derived from Latin *mulier* (woman).
*The conservative told the audience that women are importantly different from men, and should celebrate their **muliebrity** instead of talking as if it does not exist.*

mulipepantic (mū-lē-pe-PAN-tik): pertaining to sexually mature females. Derived from Latin *mulier* (woman) and Greek *pepon* (ripe).
*When the judge was caught in bed with his daughter's friend, who was seventeen, he defended himself by saying that she was obviously **mulipepantic** and fully capable of appreciating his attention.*

multicipara (multə-SIP-ə-rə): a female who has engaged in many acts of intercourse. Derived from Latin *multus* (many) and *recipere* (to receive).
*Had Monica Lewinsky not saved her stained dress in its soiled condition, she would almost certainly have been described by President Clinton's defenders as a delusional and possibly mendacious, cunning **multicipara**, or words to that effect.*

mysophilia (mī-sə-FIL-ē-ə): the tendency to become sexually aroused by smelling, chewing, or rubbing against such things as foul-smelling jock straps, bras, and panties. Derived from the Greek *mysos* (uncleanness) and *philia* (attachment, attraction).
*Because of my nephew's **mysophilia**, my family would keep the clothes hampers in a locked closet when he would visit to prevent his midnight raids.*

myzoerasty (mizō/mizǝ/mīzō-er-RASTĒ): sexual pleasure from sucking a woman's breasts; also the act of sucking breasts. Derived from Greek *myzo* (to suck) and *erastes* (lover).

Our high school gym teacher not only engaged in **myzoerasty** *with another teacher but also joked about it, saying that he finds dairy food irresistible.*

myzoeroticism (mizō/mīzǝ/mīzō-i-ROT-i-sizǝm): sexual arousal from having one's breasts sucked or suckled, as by a lover or a baby. Derived from Greek *myzo* (to suck) and *erotikos*, from *eros* (sexual love).

Bertha enjoyed **myzoeroticism** *partly because of her sensitive but not hypersensitive breasts and partly because that practice did not risk pregnancy.*

N

nanophilia (nanǝ/nanō-FIL-ē-ǝ): attraction to short people. Derived from Greek *nanos* (little old man, dwarf) and *philia* (attachment, attraction).

Because people are often attracted to their opposites, it is hardly surprising that some tall men have **nanophilia**, *and end up marrying short women.*

narcissism (NÄRSǝ-sizǝm): sexual desire for one's own body; extreme self-love. Derived from a Greek myth in which a young man, Narcissus, fell in love with his own reflection in a pool of water.

We did not understand the scope of Andy's **narcissism** *until we discovered his large number of mirrors and self-portraits.*

nasolingus (nā-zō-LING-gǝs): the act of licking or sucking someone's nose. Derived from Latin *nasus* (nose) and *lingua* (tongue).

Nasolingus *is not the safest form of sex, especially during flu season.*

nasophilia (nā-zō-FIL-ē-ǝ): arousal from seeing, touching, licking, or sucking someone's nose. Derived from Latin *nasus* (nose) and Greek *philia* (attachment, attraction).

When Durk repeatedly put chocolate syrup on Sandy's nose, and licked it off for thirty minutes, Becky learned about **nasophilia** *first hand.*

neanilagnia (nē-an-i-LAG-nē-ǝ): sexual desire for young girls. Derived from Greek *neanikos* (youthful) and *lagneia* (lust).

Woody Allen was accused of **neanilagnia** *by Mia Farrow.*

necrochlesis (nek-rō-KLĒ-sis): the molestation of a corpse. Derived from Greek *nekros* (corpse) and *ochleo* (to molest).

> *Most people find* **necrochlesis** *almost incomprehensible, since they are not in any way attracted to corpses, and do not think that such attraction is at all appropriate.*

necrocoitant (nek-rō-KŌ-i-tənt): a male who has sex with a female corpse. Derived from Greek *nekros* (dead) and Latin *coitus* (intercourse).

> *Before the* **necrocoitant** *was caught, he used to tell friends that he was planning to go to the local funeral home to pick up a few cheap dates.*

necrocoitus (kek-rō-KO-i-təs): penetration of corpses. Derived from Greek *nekros* (corpse) and Latin *coitus* (intercourse).

> *Serial killer Jeffrey Dahmer engaged in* **necrocoitus** *supposedly to exercise absolute control over people.*

necrophagia (nek-rō-FĀJ-ē-ə): cannibalism of corpses. Derived from Greek *nekros* (corpse) and *phagein* (to eat).

> *The villain Hannibal the Cannibal said that he enjoyed wine during his* **necrophagia**.

necrosadism (ne-krō-SĀ-dizəm): a pathological desire to mutilate corpses for sexual gratification. Derived from *nekros* (corpse) and *sadism* (from abusive sexual practices of aristocratic Parisian Marquis de Sade [1740–1814]).

> *We were told that the serial killer's* **necrosadism** *stemmed in part from his desire to gain pleasure while expressing rage.*

necrospermia (ne-krō-SPURM-ē-ə): a condition in which the spermatozoa in seminal fluid are immobile or dead. Derived from Greek *nekros* (corpse), the Latin combining form *-spermia* (semen) and *-ia* (suffix denoting condition).

> *The boy told his girlfriend that, because of his* **necrospermia**, *he should not need a condom.*

negative Oedipus complex: a psychoanalytic term for describing a son's experiencing sexual attraction to this father rather than his mother, as in the standard **Oedipus complex** (*see entry*). The term can also apply to a daughter's sexual attraction to her mother rather than her father, as in the standard **Electra complex** (*see entry*). The condition described is also known as an inverted Oedipus or Electra complex.

> *Because of Skippy's well-known* **negative Oedipus complex**, *he decided to run as a Democrat rather than as a Republican.*

neogamalgia (nē-ō-gə-MALJ(Ē)ə): pain attending the first act of intercourse by virginal newlyweds. Derived from Greek *neos* (new), *gamos* (marriage), and *algos* (pain).

Because of the tightness of the young bride's vagina, she experienced **neogamalgia.**

neogamosis (nē-ō-gam-MŌS-sis): frigidity in newly married women. Derived from Greek *neos* (new), *gamos* (marriage), and *-osis* (action, process, condition).

Jason was so angry with his wife because of her **neogamosis** *that he told her that her sexual inactivity was seriously threatening their marriage.*

neolagnia (nē-ō-LAG-nē-ə): the first appearance of sexual desire in females. Derived from Greek *neos* (new), *lagneia* (lust), and *-a* (feminine suffix).

Hannah was fourteen when she experienced **neolagnia,** *a state of mind simultaneously attractive and frightening to her.*

neolagnium (nē-ō-LAG-nē-əm): the first appearance of sexual desire in males. Derived from *neos* (new), *lagneia* (lust), and *-um* (masculine suffix).

Romeo was young when he experienced **neolagnium.**

nepiolagnia (nep-ē-ō-LAG-nē-ə): erotic interest in infants of the opposite sex. Derived from Greek *nepios* (infant) and *lagneia* (lust).

Parents understandably want to avoid sending their young children to any babysitter or day care provider with **nepiolagnia.**

night crawling: a sexual practice in which a young man crawls into bed with a young woman during the night without disturbing or waking the woman's family, and engages in sexual activity, including genital fondling and possibly even intercourse, depending on the culture. Though called "surreptitious rape" by anthropologist Margaret Mead, the custom can involve an invitation from a woman who wants to get a husband. Night crawling is common in Polynesian and Philippine cultures, as well as in various cultures of the Americas. In some cultures the women are the night crawlers.

Debbie's father warned her Filipino boyfriend against introducing the practice of **night crawling** *to Des Moines.*

ninety-nine: a slang term for anal intercourse, patterned on "69" (sixtynine) and synonymous with "66" (sixty-six). Supposedly, the name of Barbara Feldon's character on *Get Smart,* Agent 99, was created to suggest the number "69."

*When the football coach caught his two players performing **ninety-nine**
in the locker room, he told them that they were taking camaraderie to an
unacceptable level.*

noctorthosis (nok-tor-THŌ-sis): a nighttime erection. Derived from
Latin *nox* (night) and Greek *orthosis* (a straightening).

*Wilma told Fred that the trouble with his **noctorthosis** is that it always
shows up at night, when, unfortunately, she is too tired to be interested in
sex.*

noeclexis (nō-ek-LEKS-sis): the selection of a wife because of her intellectual capacity. Derived from Greek *noetikos* (intelligence) and *eklexis* (selection).

*G. Gordon Liddy maintains that he engaged in **noeclexis** when choosing
to take Mrs. Liddy as his bride.*

normophilia (nor-mō-FIL-ē-ə): the practice of having beliefs, attitudes,
and behavior in conformity with the standards dictated by custom or religious or civil authorities.

*The politician assured his constituents that he is a "straight shooter,"
incapable of straying from **normophilia**.*

nosophilia (nō-sə-FIL-ē-ə): arousal from believing one's sexual partner is
terminally ill. Derived from Greek *nosos* (disease) and *philia* (attachment,
attraction).

*Some men who are thought to have **nosophilia** become impotent when
their wives miraculously recover.*

notophilous (nə-TOF-i-ləs): especially attracted to female backs. Derived
from *notos* (back) and *philein* (to love).

*Until Steadman called himself a "back man," we did not realize that he
was **notophilous**.*

nubile (NOŌ-bīl): of marriageable condition or age; physically suited for,
or desirous of, a sexual relationship—especially applied to girls or young
women. Derived from Latin *nubere* (to marry).

*The recently divorced young man went out of his way to frequent places
well attended by **nubile** women.*

number three: slang for sexual intercourse.

*When American business people travel to Europe, they are sometimes told
that co-ed bathrooms are for number one and number two but not for
number three.*

nymphomania (nim(p)-fō-MĀN-ē-ə): an unusually intense sexual desire in women. Derived from Greek *nymphe* (bride, nymph) and Greek *mania* (madness, craving).

*The lustful young man told his psychology professor that **nymphomania** can definitely improve a woman's chances of getting dates.*

nymphophilia (nim(p)-fō-FIL-ē-ə): sexual attraction or attachment to a female adolescent by an adult. Derived from Greek *nymphe* (bride, nymph) and *philia* (attachment, attraction).

*We thought that Sheldon's **nymphophilia** made him unsuitable for coaching the girls' soccer team.*

O

obsidium (ob-SID-ē-um): a particular indulgence in sexual debauchery. Derived from Latin *obsidium* (a siege).

In a movie called The Rapture, *a woman desires all sorts of sex, including an **obsidium** with strangers she meets at a bar, only later to become extremely religious.*

obsolagnium (ob-sō-LAG-nē-um): the ebbing of sexual desire with advancing age. Derived from Latin *obsolescere* (to fall into disuse) and Greek *lagneia* (lust).

*The elderly man told the prostitute that she needed to leave him alone, and find someone not undergoing **obsolagnium**.*

occasional inversion: Freud's term for homosexual activity occurring when people have no access to the opposite sex for an extended time, as in prison or in the military.

*The ex-con insisted that his homosexual activity in prison was evidence of **occasional inversion** and not a general homosexual orientation.*

Oceanic position: a coital position in which the female lies on her back, and the man squats or kneels between her spread legs, usually embracing her while engaging in intercourse. The position is prevalent in the islands of the Pacific, where it is second in popularity only to the missionary position.

*Both Harry and Bess liked the **Oceanic position**, since it allowed Harry deep penetration while allowing Bess to conserve her energy.*

ochlophilia (oklə-FIL-ē-ə): sexual arousal from crowds, including orgies or large gatherings where performers and party-goers are semi-nude and pressed against one another. Derived from Greek *ochlos* (mob) and *philia* (attachment, attraction).

*We suspected John of **ochlophilia** because he always seemed a little too happy in crowded subways and elevators.*

oculolinctus (ok-ū-lō-LINK-tus): the act of licking a partner's eyeball for sexual arousal; a rare form of sex in which oral herpes can be transferred. Derived from Latin *oculus* (eye) and *lingere* (to lick).

*Prunella's opthalmologist told her that the cold sores in her eye were due to **oculolinctus**.*

odalisque (Ō-də-*lisk*): woman of a harem, as in the entourage of the Sultan of Turkey. Derived from Turkish *oda* (room) in a harem.

*The **odalisque** was presented to the Sultan by a government official.*

odaxelagnia (ō-*dak*-sə-LAG-nē-ə): a condition in which a male can achieve sexual potency only while biting his female partner, though the term can apply to women who do not enjoy intercourse unless they are bitten, or unless they bite their partners. Derived from Greek *odaxesmos* (a biting) and *lagneia* (lust).

*Mike was usually gentle when indulging his **odaxelagnia**, but this time he left teeth marks on Denise.*

odaxia (ō-DAKS-ē-ə): the biting of one's tongue or cheek during the peak of sexual excitement. Derived from Greek *odaxesmos* (a biting).

*Ginger's **odaxia** during her most recent sexual encounter caused her to injure her tongue.*

odontophilia (ō-dontə-FIL-ē-ə): sexual arousal involving teeth, possibly even including their extraction. Derived from Greek *odon* (tooth) and *philia* (attachment, attraction).

The remake of the movie Little Shop of Horrors, *starring Bill Murray, contains a sadomasochistic tooth-pulling scene possibly illustrating, among other things, **odontophilia**.*

Oedipus complex: sexual love of a son for his mother; also a son's emotional attachment to his mother accompanied by hostility toward the father. Derived from the Greek legend of Oedipus, who married his mother.

*While Matt was close to his mother, it would be unfair to say that his feelings exemplified the **Oedipus complex**.*

oenolagnia (ē-nə/nō-LAG-nē-ə): lust either induced or enhanced by alcohol, especially wine. Derived from Greek *oinos* (wine).

*Because Christopher had consumed a great deal of wine during the night he fondled his date, he ascribed his amorousness to **oenolagnia**.*

oikovalent (oi-kə-VĀL-ənt): sexually potent only in one's own home, or in a familiar environment. Derived from Greek *oikos* (home) and Latin *valere* (to be strong).

*The **oikovalent** man simply could not perform sexually in the hotel room.*

olfactolagnia (ol-fak-tō-LAG-nē-ə): sexual arousal from odors or perfumes. Derived from Latin *olfacere* (to smell) and Greek *lagneia* (lust).

*Because of Pomeroy's **olfactolagnia**, it made sense for him to join an aerobics class, where he could find a bevy of sweaty women.*

oligeunia (ol-i-GŌO-nē-ə): the practice of having sexual intercourse highly infrequently, as for lack of desire or for moral reasons. Derived from Greek *oligos* (little or scanty) and *pareunos* (para, beside and eune, bed, hence "lying beside" or "bedfellow," leading to the Greek-derived English word **pareunia** [*see entry*], sexual intercourse).

*Her friends wondered whether her **oligeunia** was due mainly to her religious upbringing, her lack of desire, or her shyness.*

oligoblysis (ol-i-gə-BLĪ/BLI-sis): a small seminal ejaculation. Derived from Greek *oligos* (few, scanty) and *blyzo* (to spurt out).

*The porn director became infuriated at the actor's **oligoblysis** and likened the sex scene to a joke without a punch line.*

olisbos (Ō-lizbəs): a device resembling the penis and used by women for masturbation; a dildo. Derived from Greek *olisbos* (penis).

*The navy wife said that she will never be unfaithful to her husband so long as she has ready access to her "second husband," an **olisbos**.*

omocoinia (omə-KOI-nē-ə): sexual intercourse without a condom, or the ability to perform or enjoy sexual intercourse only with an uncovered or "naked" organ. Derived from Greek *omos* (raw) and *koinonia* (sexual intercourse).

*Jake's mother could accept his having sex while in high school, but could not accept his occasional **omocoinia**.*

omolagnia (omə-LAG-nē-ə): erotic desire aroused by nakedness. Derived from Greek *omos* (raw) and *lagneia* (lust).

*When Ryan went skinny-dipping with Emily, he and she experienced **omolagnia**.*

oneirogmus (ō-nī-ROG-məs): an orgasm in males during sleep, especially when accompanied by an erotic dream; also known as "a wet dream." Derived from Greek *oneiros* (dream) and *ogmos* (straight or erect).
The adolescent figured that his sticky pajamas were due to his **oneirogmus**, *since he prided himself on being a tidy masturbator.*

oneiropornism (ō-nī-rō-PORN-izəm): fantasizing or dreaming about prostitutes and sex. Derived from Greek *oneiros* (dream) and *porne* (prostitute).
Roger loved to associate with prostitutes not so much to have sex with them as to stimulate images and sense impressions for his fertile imagination to translate into **oneiropornism**.

oneirotantia (ō-nī-rō-TAN-te-ə): the condition of having frequent erotic dreams, especially of naked girls tempting the dreamer to follow them. Derived from Greek *oneiros* (dream) and *Tantalus* (mythological king who was tempted with food and drink he could not reach).
After Howard's divorce his dreams took a sexual turn, giving him the experience of **oneirotantia**.

ophelimity (äf-ə-LIM-i-tē): the ability to please one's sexual partners. Derived from the Greek *ophelimos* (useful, helpful).
Many people believe that, although mutual **ophelimity** *may be necessary to many happy marriages, it is not sufficient, since sexual compatibility can rarely save a marriage that is otherwise seriously troubled.*

opsonousia (op-sō-NOO-sē-ə): the belief that the facial beauty is more important than beauty of the rest of the body. Derived from Greek *ops* (face) and *nous* (mind).
Because of his **opsonousia**, *Max easily overlooked the excess pounds of his attractive wife.*

orastorgia (ō-rə-STOR-jē-ə): the belief that true and permanent love between men and women can arise only when they are mature. Derived from Greek *oraios* (mature) and *storge* (love).
Both Kevin and his wife believed in **orastorgia**, *perhaps because both had been married several times and were now in their eighties.*

orgasmogenic (or-gaz-mə-JEN-ik): inducing or promoting orgasm. Derived from Greek *orgasmos* (swelling) and *gignesthai* (to be born).
For Don, the missionary position was optimally **orgasmogenic**.

orolabial stimulation (or-ō-LĀ-bē-əl stim-ū-LA-shən): a technical term for oral-genital contact with female genitalia; **cunnilingus** (*see entry*). Derived from Latin *or-, os* (mouth) and *labium* (lip), presumably including the suggestion of vaginal lips.

*A woman who has a firm policy to avoid kissing on the first date will probably not be open to **orolabial stimulation**.*

orthocubia (or-thə-KŪ-bē-ə): "orthodox" or conventional forms of love-making. Derived from Greek *orthos* (straight, correct) and Latin *cubare* (to lie down).

*According to some definitions (especially in certain religions), only sexual intercourse in the missionary position without "artificial" methods of birth control constitutes **orthocubia**.*

ortholagnia (or-thə/thō-LAG-nē-ə): sexual arousal from seeing an erect penis. Derived from Greek *orthos* (straight, correct) and *lagneia* (lust).

*When the young female physician excited the adolescent and herself by examining his prostrate with her finger, she assured him that her **ortholagnia** would not drive her to do anything foolish.*

orthophallic (or-thə/thō-FAL-ik): pertaining to, or having, an erection. Derived from Greek *orthos* (straight, correct), *phallos* (penis), *-ic* (adjectival ending).

*Zelda was so angry with Francis that she told him that he was useful only when he was **orthophallic**.*

orthophallogenic (or-thə/thō-fal-lō-JEN-ik): causing, or capable of causing, an erection, as in orthophallogenic photographs, movies, sex shows, and so on. Derived from Greek *orthos* (straight, correct), *phallos* (penis), and *gignesthai* (to become, to be born).

"I'll not tolerate Playboy *centerfolds or any other **orthophallogenic** pictures on my son's walls," asserted the angry mother.*

oscar: slang for a "homosexual." Derived from Oscar Wilde, author imprisoned for homosexuality in later Victorian England.

*Although the actor portrayed a womanizer on TV, a magazine revealed that he was an **oscar** in real life.*

oscarize: a slang term meaning "to have homosexual intercourse." Derived from the name of Oscar Wilde, author imprisoned for homosexuality in later Victorian England.

*When the coach caught his two track stars **oscarizing** in the locker room, they submitted that their "bonding" might have exceeded appropriate limits for their location.*

osculation (*os*-kyə-LĀ-shən): the act of kissing. Derived from Latin *osculum* (a kiss, literally "little mouth").

*When the teacher told Caleb that there shall be no **osculation** in the school hallways, he replied that he thought **osculation** was a normal process in women.*

osmolagnia (oz-mə/mō-LAG-nē-ə): sexual gratification from certain odors, including sweat and perfume. Odors, by the way, are thought to play an important role in appreciating oral sex. Derived from Greek *osme* (odor) and *lagneia* (lust).

*Bucky would reveal his **osmolagnia** by sniffing his girlfriend's genitalia for at least thirty minutes every day.*

osphresiolagniac (as/äs-frēzh-ē-ə-LAG-nē-ak): a person who is sexually aroused by odors. Derived from Greek *osphresis* (sense of smell) and *lagneia* (lust).

*As Felix was sniffing Doris's panties with evident delight, he described himself as an unregenerate **osphresiolagniac**.*

osphresiophilia (as/äs-frēzh-ē-ə-FIL-ē-ə): sexual arousal from odors or smells. Derived from Greek *osphresis* (sense of smell) and *philia* (attachment, attraction).

*Sally became a sports reporter at least partly because interviewing men in a locker room appealed to her **osphresiophilia**.*

Othello syndrome: a form of sexual paranoia in which a husband or wife is so suspicious of the spouse's possible infidelity as to be capable of fits of rage or violence. Derived from the Shakespearean character of the same name, known for having been driven into a jealous rage over his wife Desdemona, whom he kills before killing himself.

*When Kermit insisted that his wife never eat lunch with a male colleague without the presence of female colleagues, she accused him of beginning to exemplify the **Othello syndrome**.*

oxyrosis (*ok*-sē-RŌ-sis): sharpening of the sexual appetite, as because of improved fitness or health, lowered anxiety, improved sexual technique, and so on. Derived from Greek *oxys* (keen or sharp) and *eros* (sexual desire).

*Merab complimented Adriel on his **oxyrosis**, a product of his new exercise regimen.*

ozoamblyrosis (ō-zō-am-bli-RŌ-sis): loss of sexual desire or potency during sex because of bad body odor. Derived from Greek *ozo* (smell), *amblys* (dull, blunt), and *eros* (sexual desire).

The eccentric millionaire would make love to his smelly wife while he wore a gas mask to prevent ***ozoamblyrosis.***

P

pachyhymenia (pak-i-hī-MĒN-ē-ə): the condition of having a thick and tough hymen. Derived from Greek *pachy-* (thick) and *hymen* (membrane).

Rebecca's ***pachyhymenia*** *made intercourse difficult on her wedding night.*

pageism (PĀJ-izəm): masochistic sexual fantasy in which a man imagines that he is a page to a beautiful woman.

Sammy's ***pageism*** *involved infantile behavior when he would wear a diaper while slavishly following his wife's commands.*

paizocentric (*pī/pā*-zō-SEN-trik): centering one's sexual interest on foreplay. Derived from Greek *paizo* (play) and *kentron* (center of a circle).

Greg and Eileen would sometimes become frustrated, since he would like to rush to intercourse, and she would tend to be ***paizocentric.***

paizogeny (pī/pā-ZOJ-ə-nē): sexual foreplay. Derived from Greek *paizo* (play) and *genos* (race, kind, sex).

When Wally asked Ward whether he would be allowed to engage in intercourse elsewhere than at home, Ward responded that the only sex permissible for unmarried teens is ***paizogeny*** *under adult supervision.*

panerotic potential (pan-i-ROT-ik po-TEN-shəl): a theoretical belief that human beings are born with a potential for being sexually aroused by almost any person or thing until that innate potential is gradually narrowed by social influences and conditioning. Derived from Greek *pas* (all) and *eros* (sexual love).

Some religious persons who believe in the idea of ***panerotic potential*** *believe that, unless children are extensively conditioned to accept only certain forms of sexuality, they will grow into sexual anarchists.*

paneunia (pə-NO͞ON-ē-ə): sexual "promiscuity." Derived from Greek *pas* (all) and *eune* (bed).

The historian asserted that, although a number of American presidents have had mistresses at least during some periods of their lives, Presidents Kennedy and Clinton define ***paneunia.***

pansexualism: the belief that all human behavior can be explained by reference to sexual appetite. Derived from Greek *pas* (all) and Latin *sexus* (sex).
*Rightly or wrongly, many of Freud's critics accused him of **pansexualism**.*

pantagamy (pan-TAG-ə-mē): a type of group marriage within a society or community in which every adult is regarded as married to all other adults of the opposite sex. Derived from Greek *pas* (all) and *gamos* (marriage).
__Pantagamy__ is difficult to sustain because men and women often become jealous when romantically sharing their spouses.

paphian (PĀ-fē-ən): relating to illicit love; wanton. Derived from Greek *Paphos* (ancient city of Cyprus, the center of worship for Aphrodite, the goddess of love).
*The gossip columnist enjoyed writing about the **paphian** exploits of movie stars.*

pappostorgia (pap-ə-STOR-jē-ə): the belief that true and lasting love between men and women can arise only when the lovers are extremely young. Derived from Greek *pappos* (the first growth of a beard) and *storge* (love).
Roy was a romantic who found Romeo and Juliet *even more touching than most other people because of his belief in **pappostorgia**.*

paracoita (para-KŌ-i-tə): a female sex partner. Derived from Greek *para* (beside, alongside) and Latin *coitus* (sexual intercourse).
*Many Americans are deeply interested in finding out the identity of the latest **paracoita** of the most fashionable actor.*

paracoitus (para-KŌ-i-təs): a male sex partner. Derived from Greek *para* (beside, alongside) and Latin *coitus* (intercourse).
*Because Sharon was feeling extremely hungry for sex, she asked all the men at the bar whether any one of them would like to be her **paracoitus** for the night.*

paradoxia sexualis (para-DOKS-ē-ə seks-ū-AL-əs): sexual activity considered inappropriate for one's age (age-inappropriate), such as a ninety-year-old's becoming a father or a fifteen-year-old's becoming a mother. Derived from the notion of a paradox, a truth that is so ironic as to appear to be self-contradictory.
*When the actor Tony Randall became a father at seventy-odd years, at least some people thought his behavior qualified as **paradoxia sexualis**.*

paramour (PAR-ə-mǒor): a mistress or lover of either sex involved in a love affair, especially an adulterous one. Derived from the French *par amour* ("by the way of love").

*While revelations of a politician's **paramour** rarely generate much controversy any longer, a religious minister's infidelities usually do attract attention.*

parapareunia (parə-pə-ROO-ne-ə): sexual intercourse with a person who is not the usual or legal sexual partner, as when a married person has adulterous sex. Derived from Greek *para* (beside) and *pareunos* (lying beside, bedfellow).

*When he was caught in an adulterous affair, the politician warned his enemies and members of the press against treating his **parapareunia** as something important to the public or to his constituents.*

paraphallus (para-FAL-əs): an artificial penis; a dildo. Derived from Greek *para* (beside) and *phallos* (penis).

*Mary's parents were stunned to learn that Peter, supposedly the name of her boyfriend, was actually the name of her **paraphallus**.*

paraphilemia (parə-fi-LEM-e-ə): erotic kissing of body parts other than the mouth, especially the genitalia. Derived from Greek *para* (beside) and *philema* (a kiss).

*Although Fred and Joyce were open-minded, they did not think that **paraphilemia** should be presented in daytime television.*

paraphiliac (parə-FIL-e-ak): a person aroused by unconventional sexual practices. Derived from Greek *para* (beside) and *philia* (attachment, attraction).

*We did not learn that Rush was a **paraphiliac** until we discovered that he enjoyed making love in a bathtub filled with Jello.*

parascopism (parə-SKOP-izəm): an excessive desire to peep at sexual activity, as through someone else's window. Derived from Greek *para* (beside) and *skopein* (to look).

*Because we suspect that our neighbor's son was given to **parascopism**, we always keep our bedroom windows covered by blinds and draperies.*

pareunia (pə-ROO-ne-ə): sexual intercourse. Derived from Greek *pareunos*, from *para* (beside) and *eune* (lying beside, bedfellow).

*Both Ted and Alice agreed that **pareunia** was a great way for a couple to begin the day.*

pareunomania (pə-roo-nə-MAN-e-ə): a compelling urge for sexual intercourse. Derived from Greek *pareunos* (lying beside, bedfellow), *eune* (bed), and *mania* (madness, craving).

> *Pareunomania is never a sufficient justification for anyone's forcing any one else to have sex.*

pareunophrenia (pǝ-r$\overline{oo}$-nǝ-FRĒN-ē-ǝ): a mental state dominated by thoughts of, or urges for, sexual intercourse. Derived from Greek *pareunos* (lying beside, bedfellow) and *phren* (mind, diaphragm).

> *The sexologist asserted that it would be impossible to put dozens of young men and women into a room and have no one experience* **pareunophrenia**.

pareunosthenia (pǝ-r$\overline{oo}$-nǝ-S*THĒN*-ē-ǝ): male sexual vigor and ability to satisfy females. Derived from Greek *pareunos* (lying beside, bedfellow) and *sthenos* (strength).

> *Gordon has always prided himself on his* **pareunosthenia**, *especially as evidenced by his ability to please his wife.*

parhedonia (par-hē-DŌN-ē-ǝ): strong urge to touch, observe, or exhibit one's own sexual organs or those of another person. Derived from Greek *para* (beyond) and *hedone* (pleasure).

> *When asked why she, a woman with an MBA, became a stripper,* "**parhedonia**" *was her one-word reply.*

parnel (PAR-nǝl): the mistress of a priest. Derived by way of French through Latin *Petronilla* (Peter's woman).

> *If a priest is not supposed to marry, we should not be surprised by his having a* **parnel**.

parthena (par-THĒN-ǝ): virgin. Derived from Greek *parthenos* (virgin).

> *In the 1950s many young American women, before they first married, were not* **parthenas**, *and were promptly married because they had lost that status.*

parthenoclasis (par-thǝnō-KLAS-sis): sexual intercourse with a virgin; defloration. Derived from Greek *parthenos* (virgin) and *klasis* (breaking).

> *Many, but by no means all, men experience* **parthenoclasis** *during their wedding night.*

parthenoclept (par-thǝnō-KLEPT): a seducer of a virgin; a thief of virginity. Derived from Greek *parthenos* (virgin) and *klepto* (to steal).

> *Women who want to be virgins at their wedding night need to be careful to avoid* **parthenoclepts**.

parthenocolpia (par-thǝ-nō-KOLP-ē-ǝ): the condition of having a virginal vagina. Derived from Greek *parthenos* (virgin) and *kolpos* (womb, breast, vagina).

> *Once a woman loses her **parthenocolpia**, she cannot regain it.*

parthenophallic (par-thǝ-nō-FAL-ik): pertaining to male virginity, or having a virginal penis. Derived from Greek *parthenos* (virgin) and *phallos* (penis).

> *The author and playwright George Bernard Shaw was **parthenophallic** until he was twenty-nine, according to his own testimony.*

parthenophile (par-THĒNǝ-fīl): a male who is attracted only to virgins. Derived from Greek *parthenos* (virgin) and *philein* (to love).

> *Since Grace has slept with many boys, Calvin, a **parthenophile**, has no interest in her.*

parthenophobia (par-thǝnō/thǝnǝ-FŌB-ē-ǝ): a morbid fear of virgins. Derived from Greek *parthenos* (virgin) and *phobos* (fear).

> *Hugh Hefner, the founder of* Playboy *magazine, probably has no sexual fears, except possibly **parthenophobia**.*

partialism: intense sexual interest in one part of the body, as when people are "turned on" by legs, feet, breasts, hairy chests, and so on.

> *Beulah feared that Buster's **partialism** had reached new heights—or depths—when he started licking the smallest toe on her left foot.*

particular friendship: a euphemism for an exclusive and emotional friendship between members of the same sex that is assumed to be sexual or potentially sexual. Historically, officials within Roman Catholic seminaries and convents warned against what they described as the dangers of particular friendships.

> *Some people worry that they may have sexual feelings in relationships that would be condemned as **particular friendships** by certain religious authorities.*

partousse (par-TŌOS): a French term meaning, almost literally, an "orgy" or "group sex."

> *When Roger's fellow workers learned that his last party included a **partousse**, he suddenly became popular.*

paternorexis (pa-tur-nǝ-REKS-sis): the sexual love of a daughter for her father. Derived from Latin *pater* (father) and Latin/Greek *orexis* (appetite).

> *We assured the cynical adolescent that, while the character of Kathy*

"Kitten" Anderson on the TV show Father Knows Best *loved her father, her feelings did not qualify as* **paternorexis**.

pecattiphilia (pe-kat-i-FIL-ē-ə): sexual arousal from sinning. Some teenagers who have grown up in religious homes enjoy masturbation at least partly because it is forbidden. Sometimes people will derive pleasure from performing acts that intensify feelings of guilt, as when they seduce virgins, wear religious costumes or symbols, listen to hymns during sex, or even have sex in church. Persons suffering from extreme pecattiphilia might ask their partners to punish them before they achieve orgasm. Derived from Latin *peccatum* (sin) and Greek *philia* (attachment).

> *Because of Tommy's* **pecattiphilia***, he would have sex soon after hearing a sermon condemning it.*

pectotage (PEK-tə-täzh): sexual manipulation of the female breasts, especially as part of foreplay. Derived from Latin *pectus* (breast) and French *barboter* (to splash about).

> *Paul would combine* **pectotage** *with silliness as he would treat his wife's breasts as gear shifts.*

pederosis (ped-e-RŌS-sis): erotic love for children; molestation of children. Derived from Greek *pais* (child) and *-osis* (state, process, condition).

> *The accusations of* **pederosis** *did not help Michael Jackson's image.*

pedihapsis (ped-i-HAP-sis): the erotic or amorous touching of a child. Derived from Greek *pais* (child) and *haptein* (to fasten).

> *Sometimes a teacher will innocently touch a child, and that contact will be misinterpreted as* **pedihapsis**.

pediochlesis (ped-ē-ō/ə-KLĒ-sis): molestation of children. Derived from Greek *pais* (child) and *ochleo* (to molest).

> *Americans will generally disapprove of* **pediochlesis** *because they know how psychologically fragile children can be.*

pedomentia (ped-ə/ō-MEN-tē-ə): the popular but baseless belief that the size of a man's sexual organ can be estimated from the size of his feet. Derived from Latin *pedis* (foot) and *mentula* (penis).

> *The basketball player with size eighteen shoes profited from a widespread belief in* **pedomentia**.

pedophthoria (ped-ō-FTHOR-rē-ə): in ancient Greece, the sexual seduction of boys by adult men. Derived from Greek *phthoria* (corruption) and *pais* (child).

The dean of the all-male academy assured parents that pedophthoria
will not be tolerated on his campus.

Peggy Lee syndrome: feelings of disappointment reported by teenaged
girls on their first occasion of sexual intercourse. Derived by sexologist
David Weis from Peggy Lee's popular song, *Is That All There Is?*
Because Faye expected fireworks to go off during her first taste of
intercourse, her experiencing the **Peggy Lee syndrome** *was almost*
inevitable.

penectomy (pe-NEK-tō-me, pen-EK-tō-mē): removal of the penis.
Derived from Latin *penis* (tail, penis), *-ectomia* from Greek *ek-* (out), and
tomos (a cutting).
Whenever Duane would say unkind things to his wife, she would pull out
a knife and threaten him with a **penectomy***.*

penilingus (pen-i-LING-gəs): derived from Greek *peos* (penis) and Latin
lingere (to lick).
The priest warned the married couple against "unnatural sex," including
penilingus*, which he said involved the unnatural use of at least two*
organs.

penis captivus (PĒN-is kap-TĒ-vus): retention of the penis within the
vagina because of vaginismus or the painful spasm of the vagina, a condition that is more likely to occur in animals than in human beings. Derived
from Latin *captivus* (prisoner).
When Bubba said that he had experienced penis captivus *with his wife,*
she countered that she could never have trapped something too small to see.

penorthosis (pen-or-THŌ-sis): an erection. Derived from Latin *penis*
(penis, tail), akin to Greek *peos* (penis), and Greek *orthos* (straight).
Jimmy, who was wearing tight slacks, felt embarrassed by his
penorthosis*.*

penultima (pi-NUL-tə-mə, pi-nul-TĒ-mə): a woman who freely engages
in sex play but stops short of the last act (sexual intercourse). (*See also* **demi-
vierge***.*) Derived from the Latin *paene* (almost) and *ultimus* (last).
The man said that he did not want a **penultima***, but a woman who*
would consummate their relationship.

peotillomania (pē-ō-til-ō-MĀN-ē-ə): the neurotic habit of constantly
pulling at one's penis. Derived from Greek *peos* (penis), *tillo* (to pluck), and
mania (madness, craving).

Johnson's **peotillomania** *was less noticeable on the baseball diamond than it was at the formal ball, where men are expected to keep their hands away from their private parts.*

peotomy (pē-OT-ō-mē): amputation of the penis. Derived from Greek *peos* (penis) and *tomos* (cutting, from *temnein*, to cut).

Although Duane was given a **peotomy** *by his angry and abused wife, he was still able to star in a porn film some time later.*

perdurothosis (pur-durō-THŌ-sis): condition of having a long-lasting male erection. Derived from Latin *perdurare* (to endure) and Greek *orthos* (straight).

A man's capacity for **perdurothosis** *is important for many female sexual partners and essential for porn stars.*

perineum (*pār*-ə-NĒ-əm): the area between the anus and the scrotum of a male, or between the anus and the vagina of the female. Derived from Greek *perinaion: peri-* (near, about) and *inein* (to empty out).

The **perineum** *is sometimes known by the slang term "taint" because "it ain't" the anus or the scrotum on a male, or the anus or the vagina on a female.*

phallacrasia (fala-KRAZ-ē-ə, fala-KRĀ-zhə): excessive sexual use of the penis. Derived from Greek *phallos* (penis) and *akrasia* (incontinence).

When Mary Ellen learned about Eddie's **phallacrasia**, *she asked Wally to protect her from Eddie's lustful advances.*

phallalingus (fa-lə-LING-gəs): licking of the penis. Derived from Greek *phallos* (penis) and Latin *lingere* (to lick).

Michelle found it easy to fit **phallalingus** *into her busy schedule, since it required little time, and did not require her to get undressed.*

phallata (fal-LOT-ə): a female who has had sexual intercourse. Derived from Greek *phallos* (penis) and *-a* (a feminine suffix).

Like many men, Howard wanted to date a **phallata**, *but marry a virgin.*

phallate (FAL-āt): to insert the male sexual organ into the vagina and to perform intercourse; copulate. Derived from Greek *phallos* (penis).

A number of young Americans believe that oral sex is not genuine sex because they believe that in genuine sex people must **phallate**.

phallesthesia (fal-es-THĒ-zhə, fal-es-THĒZ-ē-ə): the feeling or illusion that one has a phallus, as experienced by some hysterical women. Derived from Greek *phallos* (penis) and *aistheses* (feeling).

*Because the conservative Republican saw Hillary Clinton's assertiveness as obnoxiously mannish, he accused her of **phallesthesia**.*

phallic anabasis (FAL-ik ə-NAB-ə-sis): the process of becoming erect, as applied to the male organ. Derived from Greek *phallos* (penis) and *anabainein* (to go up).
*Desmond was unusual enough to experience **phallic anabasis** simply by hearing his wife pass gas.*

phallic catabasis (FAL-ik kə-TAB-ə-sis): the process of becoming flaccid, as applied to the erect male organ. Derived from Greek *katabainein* (to go down).
*Mortimer's wife would complain that the one-minute interim between his erection and his **phallic catabasis** frustrated her libido.*

phallic impaction (FAL-ik im-PAK-shən): a condition in which the male erection becomes so tightly wedged in the vagina as to make withdrawal difficult or impossible. The condition can arise when the male organ is much too large for the vagina, or when the vagina has spasms. Derived from Greek *phallos* (penis) and Latin *impactus* (lodgement).
*John thought that **phallic impaction** was possible only in certain nonhuman animals, and was deeply humiliated when paramedics had to separate him and his girlfriend.*

phallocacosis (falə-ka-KŌ-sis): the belief by a man that his sexual organ is repulsive to women. Derived from Greek *phallos* (penis) and *kakos* (bad).
*Because of Gomer's **phallocacosis**, he was afraid to disrobe on his wedding night.*

phallocrypsis (fa-lə-KRIP-sis): retraction of the penis to a point at which it becomes nearly invisible. Derived from Greek *phallos* (penis) and *kryptos* (hidden).
*Because of Ray's small penis and his **phallocrypsis**, his wife complained that sex with him involved playing hide-and-seek.*

phallodynia (fa-lə-DĪN-ē-ə): a medical term for a pain in the penis. Derived from Greek *phallos* (penis) and *dye* (pain).
*Jill told Jack that, if he had not tried to have sex with her while they were rolling down the hill, perhaps he would not be experiencing **phallodynia**.*

phallohapsis (fa-lə-HAP-sis): the caressing of the phallus. Derived from Greek *phallos* (penis) and *haptein* (to fasten).

*Many women can be quite satisfied with hugging their partners and
engaging in **phallohapsis** without receiving penetration of any kind.*

phallohaptate (falə-HAP-tāt): to caress the penis. Derived from Greek
phallos (penis) and *haptein* (to fasten).

*Women who do not believe that oral sex is really sex will certainly believe
that to **phallohaptate** a male also does not involve sex.*

phallolalia (fa-lə-LĀL-ē-ə): obscene conversation about penises. Derived
from the Greek *phallos* (penis) and *lalia* (talk, chatter).

*The careful politician told his constituents that he would fire any aides
who engaged in **phallolalia** unless they were seriously discussing a
medical condition.*

phallomaniac (fa-lə/lō-MĀN-ē-ak): a woman "crazy about" penises.
Derived from Greek *phallos* (penis) and *mania* (madness, craving).

*Any woman who always wants to have two males penetrate each of her
orifices at the same time is likely to be described as a **phallomaniac**.*

phallomeiosis (fa-lə-mī-Ō-sis): a man's belief (possibly erroneous) that his
penis is too small for effective intercourse. Derived from Greek *phallos*
(penis) and *meioun* (to diminish).

*We told our friend David that, unfortunately, there was a factual basis
for his **phallomeiosis**, and that a penile pump would not help him
permanently to enlarge his tiny organ.*

phalloperissia (fa-lə-pur-IZ-ē-ə): excessive preoccupation with the male
sexual organ. Derived from Greek *phallos* (penis) and *perisseia* (abundance,
surplus); related to *perissos* (extraordinaire).

*When Monica's mother saw thirty dildos, a dozen squash, and two
hundred condom-covered bananas in her daughter's room, she suspected
Monica of **phalloperissia**.*

phalloperosis (fa-lə-pur-Ō-sis): malicious mutilation or amputation of
the penis. Derived from *phallos* (penis) and *perosis* (malicious mutilation).

*Once a wife becomes so angry with her husband as to commit
phalloperosis, their marriage is very likely at a breaking point.*

phallophilia (falə-FIL-ē-ə): attraction to, and arousal from, erect penises
of extraordinary size or endurance. Derived from Greek *phallos* (penis) and
philia (attachment, attraction).

*Brenda's **phallophilia** prompted her to brag about her well-endowed
husband.*

phallophobia (falə-FŌB-ē-ə): fear of erections. Derived from Greek *phallos* (penis) and *phobos* (fear).

*Because of Janet's **phallophobia**, she asked that her husband always have his pants on around her.*

phallorthific (fal-lor-THI-fik): causing, or capable of causing, an erection. Derived from the Greek *phallos* (penis), Greek *orthos* (straight), and Latin *-fic*, from *facere* (to make).

*The politician told his friends that he finds young women in thongs **phallorthific.***

phallosugia (fal-ə-SOŌ-jē-ə): erotic sucking of the penis. Derived from Greek *phallos* (penis) and Latin *sugo* (to suck).

*Chastity likes answering the phone in the middle of sex, except when she's performing **phallosugia**.*

phanermania (fan-ur-MĀN-ē-ə): an irresistible impulse to touch or stroke a part of one's own body, especially a protruding part, such as a nose or breast. The compulsion usually has a sexual meaning for the person. Derived from the Greek *phaner(o)-* (visible) and *mania* (madness, craving).

*George's unremittingly stroking his nose while watching pornographic films suggested to us **phanermania**.*

pherbasia (fur-BĀZH-ə, fur-BĀZH-ē-ə): a kiss endured without obvious opposition, but eliciting no response. Derived from the Greek *phero* (to bear or endure) and Latin *basium* (a kiss).

*Her kiss was devoid of passion, a mere **pherbasia**.*

philemacentric (fil-ə-mə-SEN-trik): centering one's erotic attentions on kissing. Derived from Greek *philema* (kiss) and *kentron* (center of a circle).

*Many people, especially women, are **philemacentric**, finding passionate kissing the most sexually stimulating activity.*

philemagenic (fil-ə-mə-JEN-ik): inciting or inducing a desire to kiss. Derived from Greek *philema* (a kiss) and *gignesthai* (to be born).

*Jack found Jill's licking her lips highly **philemagenic**.*

philemalgia (fil-ə-MAL-j(ē)ə): the condition of being unresponsive or cold to kissing. Derived from the Greek *philema* (a kiss) and Latin *algidus* (cold).

*Since George regarded kissing as an essential prelude to romance, he had no patience with women affected by **philemalgia**.*

philemamania (fil-ə-mə-MĀN-ē-ə): an intense desire to kiss. Derived from Greek *philema* (a kiss) and *mania* (madness, craving).
Joan looked so beautiful to Edgar that he could no longer resist his **philemamania**, *and gave her the most passionate kiss she had ever had.*

philemaphile (FIL-ə-mə-fīl): a person fond of kissing. Derived from Greek *philema* (a kiss) and *philein* (to love).
Since both Tarzan and Jane are **philemaphiles**, *they spend more time kissing than expressing their feelings for each other in other ways.*

philemaphobe (FIL-ə-mə-fōb): a person who fears or dislikes kissing. Derived from *philema* (a kiss) and *phobos* (fear).
Johnny was a **philemaphobe** *who preferred sexual intercourse to kissing.*

philemaxenosis (fil-ə-maks-ə/ē-NŌ-sis): the practice of unorthodox kissing, especially in the choice of the body part that is kissed, such as the nipple, foot, or buttocks. Derived from the Greek *philema* (a kiss), *xenos* (a stranger), and *-osis* (condition).
One of Bill Clinton's advisors was known for his **philemaxenosis**, *as when he kissed prostitute's toes.*

philemorthotic (fil-ə-mor-THOT-tik): preferring, or tending, to kiss in the customary way. Derived from Greek *philema* (a kiss) and *orthos* (straight, correct).
The grandiloquent conservative talk show host told his listeners that, refreshingly, President George W. Bush is a **philemorthotic** *paragon of patriotism, not a perjurious pervert.*

philemyosis (fil-ə-mī-Ō-sis): kissing while the eyes are kept shut. Derived from the Greek *philema* (a kiss) and *myo* (to keep one's eyes shut).
Some people insist that they enjoy **philemyosis** *because it enables them to focus more closely on the feel of the kiss.*

philoboupaes (fil-ə-BŌŌ-pa-es): in ancient Greece, an adult man who is sexually interested in big or bulky boys. Derived from the Greek *philein* (to love) and *bous* (ox).
When the high school football coach referred to his athletes as "strapping young bucks," we came close to believing that he was a **philoboupaes**.

philomeirax (fil-ə-MĪ-raks): in ancient Greece, a mature man who loves boys in their prime. The tragedian Sophocles was called a philomeirax, regarded as term of praise. Derived from the Greek *philein* (to love) and *meirax* (beautiful).

*Some of Hollywood's most famous male sex symbols were either bisexuals or **philomeiraxes**.*

philomolysmist (fil-ǝ-mō-LIZ-mist): lover of obscenity in any form. Derived from the Greek *philein* (to love), *molysma* (pollution), and *-ist* (one who).

*Whether the radio "shock jock" Howard Stern simply gives people what they want, or whether he is a **philomolysmist** who knows how to capitalize on what he likes, is hard to tell.*

philopornist (fil-ǝ-PORN-ist): lover of "loose women" or prostitutes. Derived from the Greek *porne* (a prostitute), *philein* (to love), and *-ist* (one who).

*Although the evangelist did not describe himself as a **philopornist**, he did admit to having relations with a prostitute.*

phrenapistia (frenǝ-PIS-tē-ǝ): spiritual or mental sexual unfaithfulness to one's spouse, as when people have lust in their hearts or engage in erotic daydreaming. Derived from Greek *phren* (mind, diaphragm) and *apistia* (unfaithfulness).

*When former president Jimmy Carter admitted to having lusted in his heart, he might have been confessing to something approaching **phrenapistia**.*

piblokto (pi-BLOK-tō): an acute hysterical state in which Eskimo women scream, tear off their clothes, and run around naked in the snow while making bird or other animal sounds. The behavior is thought to stem from frustration and sexual abuse. Derived from the Inuit *pibloktoq*.

*The anthropologist explained that conduct characteristic of **piplokto** does not express sexual abandon, but the extreme frustration some Eskimo women feel.*

picket-fence injury: medical jargon for a vaginal injury resulting from inserting foreign objects during masturbation. Derived from its resemblance to the shape of a picket fence.

*After examining Bertha's **picket-fence injury**, her physician told her and her husband that the vagina is not a cubby hole for placing light bulbs and sharp objects.*

pleoblysis (plēō-BLĪ/BLI-sis): a copious seminal ejaculation. Derived from Greek *pleion* (more) and *blyzo* (to spurt out).

*After Peter's **pleoblysis** during the climatic scene of his first porn movie, the producer hired him for a series of movies.*

podophilemia (podō-fə-LĒM-ē-ə): the act of deriving pleasure from kissing a woman's feet. Derived from Greek *pous* (foot) and *philemia* (a kiss).
Monty would thoroughly wash Natalie's feet before engaging in ***podophilemia***.

podophilia (podō-FIL-ē-ə): attraction to, or arousal from, feet. Derived from Greek *pous* (foot) and *philia* (attachment, attraction).
We suspected Mortimer of ***podophilia*** *when we realized that the only photographs he had of his wife were of her bare feet while one foot was pumping the accelerator of the family truck.*

polyiterophilia (polē-it-ur-ō-FIL-ē-ə): a condition in which people need to repeat the same sexual activity several times before they can achieve orgasm or satisfaction. Derived from Greek *polys* (many), Latin *itero* (repeat), and Greek *philia* (attachment, attraction).
When Chris told us that he felt a need to masturbate at least six times a day, we told him that he might consider seeking help for his ***polyiterophilia***.

polymorphous perverse (polē-MOR-fus pur-VURS): Freud's term for the capacity to respond to diverse forms or sources of sexual stimulation, such as sucking, masturbating, viewing, smelling, and defecating. The capacity originates in infancy and is exercised to some extent in "normal" sexual activity, though it can also take the form of unconventional sexual practices. Derived from the Greek *polymorphos* (multiform) and the Latin *perversus* (facing the wrong way).
Anyone who does not know what it means to be ***polymorphous perverse*** *need only pick up a catalog of sexual supplies, where the person will find numerous ointments, nipple clips, butt plugs, and other things many people have never heard of.*

pornephilia (por-nə-FIL-ē-ə): either a fondness for, or a preoccupation with, prostitutes. Derived from Greek *porne* (prostitute) and *philia* (attachment, attraction).
Many politicians appear to display a ***pornephilia***, *perhaps stemming from a realization that they and prostitutes share a similar line of work.*

pornocracy (por-NOK-kru-sē): government by prostitutes. Derived from Greek *porne* (prostitute) and *kratos* (power).
Many people regard our form of government as a ***pornocracy*** *in which politicians prostitute themselves.*

pornographomania (porn-ō-graf-ə-MĀN-ē-ə): a compulsion to write sexually obscene material, especially letters. Derived from Greek *porne* (prostitute), *graphein* (to write), and *mania* (madness, craving).

*The religious parents believed that most computer chat rooms are simply vehicles for **pornographomania**.*

pornolagnia (porn-ō/ə-LAG-nē-ə): an extreme attraction to prostitutes and to sexual activity with them. Derived from Greek *porne* (prostitute) and *lagneia* (lust).

*It is remarkable how famous or powerful men who can have anyone they want sexually often feel the need to pay women to indulge the men's **pornolagnia**.*

postillionnage (pos-til-yon-ÄZH): a French word for inserting and manipulating a finger in the anus of one's partner during foreplay, or intercourse, or in one's own anus during masturbation.

*A person can rarely overestimate the value of a deftly placed finger, or so say practitioners of **postillionnage**.*

priapism (PRĪ-ə-*piz*-əm): a persistent and often painful erection, more usually a product of disease than sexual arousal. Derived from the Greek *Priapos*, the Greek god of procreation and the personification of the erect phallus.

*The young man assured his peers that his **priapism** was not enjoyable but unpleasant, and a product of a medical condition.*

primesodia (prim-ə-SŌD-ē-ə): a female's first act of sexual intercourse. Derived from Latin *primus* (first) and Greek *eisodos* (a coming in).

*Many if not most women vividly remember their **primesodia**, even if that experience occurred decades ago.*

primesodophobia (prim-ə-sō-dō-FŌB-ē-ə): a female's morbid fear of her first act of intercourse. Derived from Latin *primus* (first), Greek *eisodos* (a coming in), and Greek *phobos* (fear).

*Given the psychological fragility of many young women, **primesodophobia** is quite understandable.*

proctophobia (prok-tō-FŌB-ē-ə): fear of, or aversion to, any erotic contact with the rectum. Derived from the Greek *proktos* (rectum) and *phobos* (fear).

*Danny was disturbed by his wife's **proctophobia**, since he was convinced that every orifice has a valuable role in loveplay.*

pseudocopulation (soo-dō-kop-ū-LĀ-shən): physical contact between a male and female producing excitement and orgasm without intercourse. Derived from Greek *pseudo* (false) and Latin *copulare* (to bind or join).
The high school students would often engage in **pseudocopulation** *because of their fear of pregnancy.*

pseudohermaphroditism (soo-dō-hər-MAF-rə-dī-*tiz*-əm): a congenital condition in a person who has either testes or ovaries as well as the external genitalia of the opposite sex. Derived from Greek *pseudo* (false) and the Greek god *Hermaphroditos* (Hermes and Aphrodite), the son of Hermes and Aphrodite who became united in one body with the nymph Salmacis.
Jerry's **pseudohermaphroditism** *confused his sexual partners, since he had a deep voice and a hairy chest, but a vagina.*

pseudomacrophallia (soo-dō-makrō-FAL-ē-ə): the condition of having a penis that appears large when flaccid but does not increase much in size when it becomes erect. Derived from Greek *pseudo* (false), *makros* (long), and *phallos* (penis).
Because of his **pseudomacrophallia**, *Bobby would tell his sexual partners after he and they would undress, "This is about as good as it gets."*

pseudomicrophallia (soo-dō-mīkrō-FAL-ē-ə): the condition of having a penis that appears unusually small when flaccid but becomes remarkably large when erect. Derived from Greek *pseudo* (false), *makros* (long), and *phallos* (penis).
Because of Ronald's **pseudomicrophallia**, *his sexual partners would first laugh at his tiny flaccid male organ, but then gasp at its tumescent length, right after his customary remark, "You ain't seen nothing yet."*

pseudovoyeurism (soo-dō-voi-YUR-izəm, soo-dō-vwa-YUR-izəm): a mild form of voyeurism in which the voyeur would prefer heterosexual sex simply to watching nude people, as distinguished from true voyeurism, in which the voyeur prefers looking to participating. Derived from Greek *pseudo* (false) and French *voir* (to see).
When his girlfriend was unavailable for lovemaking, John would resort to **pseudovoyeurism**.

psychic masturbation: sexual gratification achieved through erotic fantasies and without genital manipulation.

*Carl's capacity for generating intensely erotic mental imagery enabled him to enjoy **psychic masturbation**.*

psychrocism (SĪ-krō-sizəm): arousal from either being cold, or watching someone else who is cold. Derived from Greek *psychros* (cold).

*Elwood's **psychrocism** would lead him to put a towel into the freezer, and then lay it on his genitals before he would have sex.*

pubic wig: a hair piece worn by women on the pubic area, especially in seventeenth-century England; also called a **merkin** (*see entry*).

***Pubic wigs** were especially fashionable in seventeenth-century England.*

pygobombe (PĪ-gō-bom): a female with well-rounded buttocks, often oscillating as she walks. Derived from Greek *pyge* (buttocks) and French *bombe* (rounded or bulging).

*Many people regard singer Jennifer Lopez as quite the **pygobombe**.*

pygomania (*pi*-gə-MĀN-ē-ə): obsession with female buttocks. Derived from Greek *pyge* (buttocks) and *mania* (madness, craving).

*We learned about Desmond's **pygomania** when he told us that he prefers women with shapely but substantial rumps.*

pygophilemia (pī-gə-fi-LĒM-ē-ə): act of deriving satisfaction from kissing female buttocks. Derived from Greek *pyge* (buttocks) and *philema* (a kiss).

*Because most men are attracted to the female rump, it is hardly surprising that many men enjoy **pygophilemia**.*

pygophilous (pī-GOF-ə-ləs): being especially attracted to female buttocks. Derived from Greek *pyge* (buttocks) and *philein* (to love).

*Because Nelson was **pygophilous**, he could hardly keep his hands off Jeanette's buttocks.*

pygosemantics (pī-gə-si-MAN-tiks): the universal language of swaying hips and oscillating buttocks. Derived from Greek *pyge* (buttocks) and *semantikos* (significant).

*Tony would always sit at the back of the class because of his interest in **pygosemantics**.*

pygotripsis (pī-gə-TRIP-sis): the sexual practice in which two or more persons rub their buttocks together. Derived from the Greek *pyge* (buttocks) and *tripsis* (a rubbing).

When the football coach discovered two players in the locker room engaged in **pygotripsis**, *he told them that they were taking their positions as tight ends way too literally.*

pyrolagnia (pī-rə-LAG-nē-ə): sexual arousal from observing fires. Derived from Greek *pyros* (fire) and *lagneia* (lust).

People with **pyrolagnia** *often have special radios enabling them to pick up reports of current fires so that they can watch the blazes.*

Q

quatiosis (kwod-tē-Ō-sis): the practice of a woman's arousing a man's sexual appetite by shaking parts of her body. Derived from Latin *quatio* (to shake) and *-osis* (condition).

The man frequented strip clubs because of his attraction to **quatiosis**.

quatopygia (kwod-tə-PIJ/PĪJ-ē-ə): the shaking of the buttocks in walking, a word applied especially to an erotic feminine walk. Derived from the Latin *quatio* (to shake) and Greek *pyge* (buttocks).

Once on a Hawaiian beach, Greg Brady, of The Brady Bunch, *chose to lie down to enjoy watching beautiful women and their* **quatopygia**.

quean (kwēn): a prostitute. Derived from Middle English *quean*, from Old English *cwene* (woman).

Most **queans** *will not immediately offer their services for money, but will instead ask men whether they would like dates.*

queening (KWĒN-ing): the European practice of a dominant female using a man's head or face as a throne by sitting either on the side of his head or on his face as a bondage technique. Derived from the royal practice of sitting on real thrones.

The chief executive officer of our company was reputed to enjoy passive sex and to prefer females who delight in **queening**.

quim: a vernacular term from the seventeenth to the twentieth centuries for the female genitalia.

The pornographer Larry Flynt once said that the **quim** *is the sexiest part of a woman's body.*

quim-stick: obsolete slang for penis. Derived from adding "stick" to the vernacular term **quim** (*see entry*), the female genitalia.

*Many public figures get into trouble because they have trouble controlling their **quim-sticks**.*

R

rantallion (ran-TAL-ē-ən, ran-TAL-yən): a man or boy whose scrotum hangs lower than his penis; one "whose short pouch is longer than the barrel of his piece," in Sir Francis Grose's *1811 Dictionary of the Vulgar Tongue*.
*The porn director, who described himself as a genital aesthete, put up a sign on the door of his studio that read: "Actors and models wanted: **Rantallions** need not apply."*

rectalgia (rek-TAL-j(ē)ə): pain in the rectum. Derived from Latin *rectus* (straight) and Greek *algos* (pain).
*In her interview, the porn star said that she would do anything except what would give her **rectalgia**.*

recumbofavia (rə-kum-bō-FAV/FĀV-ē-ə): a preference for reclining during sexual intercourse. Derived from Latin *recumbere* (to lie or recline) and *faveo* (to favor).
*Mickey's **recumbofavia** was due not so much to a positive preference as to a lack of energy and imagination.*

renifleur (ren-ə-FLəR/FLIRRH): one who receives sexual gratification from smells, as of urine. Derived from French *renifler* (to sniff).
*The **renifleur** was a medical lab technician who was more than a little enthusiastic around urine specimens.*

rhabdolagnia (rab-dō/də-LAG-nē-ə): sexual arousal from either beating a person with a cane, or (less usually) being beaten with a cane. Derived from Greek *rhabdos* (rod) and *lagneia* (lust).
*The young wife used to refer to her first husband as "Citizen Kane" because of his **rhabdolagnia**.*

rheononia (rēō-NŌN-ē-ə): a form of female masturbation in which a stream of water, as from a faucet or rubber hose, is directed at the vagina. Derived from Greek *rheos* (anything flowing, including a stream) and *koinonia* (intercourse).
*The puritanical mother would insist that her daughter take no baths but only five-minute showers to decrease her daughter's opportunity for **rheononia**.*

Roman culture: a colloquial term for orgies and "swinging" (exchanging sexual partners) derived from similar practices of sexual indulgence within certain circles of ancient Rome.

In the world of classified personal ads, persons who sincerely express an interest in Roman culture may care little for Italy or ancient Rome, but are attracted to group sex.

S

sacofricosis (sakə/sakō-fri-KŌ-sis): the practice of a male's handling his genitalia through an opening cut in his pants pocket while being in public, presumably to appear only semi-disgusting; in slang, the practice is called "pocket pool." Derived from Latin *sacculus* (pocket, small bag) and *fricare* (to rub).

The mayor said that he will not tolerate sacrofricosis in Central Park, even if that means arresting all males walking with hands in their pockets.

saliromania (sa-ler-o-MĀN-ē-ə): compulsion to gain sexual arousal from preoccupation with filth, ugliness, or deformity, as when people enjoy soiling their sexual partners, smelling anal or urinary ordors, or watching mud wrestling. Derived from Latin *salinus* (of salt) and Greek *philia* (attachment, attraction).

When the maid noticed John's soiled bed sheets, he told her that he had experienced an accident, but we suspected that he and his wife were unusual enough to indulge their saliromania.

salirophilia (sa-ler-o-FIL-ē-ə): attraction to tasting salty bodily secretions, such as sweat. Derived from Latin *salinus* (of salt) and Greek *philia* (attachment, attraction).

When Jerry was licking Lucia's sweaty arm, we learned of his salirophilia.

sapphism (SAF-izəm): sexual desire of one woman for another; lesbianism. Derived from the ancient Greek, *Sappho* of Lesbos, known for her lesbian poetry.

According to radio talk show host Neal Boortz, sapphism is extremely common among female strippers, who are often more interested in one another than in their male audience.

sapphismolagny (saf-iz-mə-LAG-nē): male sexual gratification from thinking about, reading, or watching lesbian activities. Derived from Greek poet *Sappho* of Lesbos (about 600 B.C.) and Greek *lagneia* (lust).

Sapphismolagny is so common that lesbian sex is considered standard fare in heterosexual pornography, and suggestions of lesbianism have become increasingly common in ordinary movies.

sappholinction (saf-ə/ō-LINK-shən): the licking of female genitalia by females; cunnilingus performed by lesbians. Derived from ancient Greek poetess Sappho and Latin *lingere* (to lick).

Sappholinction appeals to many men largely because cunnilingus and women appeal to them.

sarmassophilia (sar-*mas*-ə-FIL-ē-ə): a fondness for amorously touching females, especially kneading their breasts. Derived from Greek *sarx* (flesh), *masso* (to knead), and *philia* (attachment, attraction).

*A highly tactile person, Melissa enjoyed providing her breasts to satisfy her husband's **sarmassophilia**.*

satyriasis (sā-tə-RĪ-ə-sis): excessive, often considered uncontrollable, sexual desire in males. Derived from Greek *satyros* (Satyr, Greek mythological woodland creature depicted as having pointed ears, legs, and short horns of a goat and an attraction to unrestrained revelry).

The movie Carnal Knowledge *starred Jack Nicholson, who played a character with **satyriasis**.*

scatography (ska-TOG-rə-fē): the practice of writing material, including graffiti, regarding functions of elimination, to express or arouse sexual interest. Derived from Greek *skatos* (excrement) and *graphein* (to write).

*Some critics regard Howard Stern's books as little more than **scatography**.*

scatology (ska-TOL-ə-jē): obscene literature; interest in things filthy or obscene. Derived from Greek *skatos* (excrement) and *logos* (word, reason, speech).

Although many people praise the artistry of D. H. Lawrence's Sons and Lovers, *many people used to disparage it as **scatology**.*

schizerastia (ski-zur-RAS-tē-ə): sexual arousal from gazing at a woman's cleavage. Derived from Greek *schizein* (to split), *erastes* (lover), and *skopein* (to view).

*Whenever Raymond was near a woman with a low-cut dress, his manifest **schizerastia** would embarrass her.*

scopophilia (skō-pə-FIL-ē-ə): a desire to look at others' sexual activities or organs, especially as a substitute for sexual participation. Derived from Greek *skopein* (to view) and *philia* (attachment).

People affected by **scopophilia** *are amply satisfied with attending orgies simply to watch.*

scoptolagnia (skop-tō-LAG-nē-ə): sexual arousal from looking at nude persons or exposed genitalia. Derived from Greek *skopein* (to look) and *lagneia* (lust).

A porn movie entitled I Like To Watch *deals with* **scoptolagnia.**

secret vice: a Victorian expression for masturbation.

Whenever Marvin would become sexually frustrated, he would retire to the closet, shut the door, and indulge in the **secret vice.**

self-pollution: an old derogatory term for masturbation, regarded as a dirty habit of self-abuse.

Former U.S. Surgeon General Joycelyn Elders regarded masturbation not as **self-pollution,** *but as a form of safe and wholesome sex.*

sempereria (sem-pə-RĀR-ē-ə): the quality of having an everlasting capacity to arouse male lust, possessed, for example, by certain famous stars. Derived from Latin *semper* (always) and Greek *eros* (sexual love).

The **sempereria** *of actresses Grace Kelly and Marilyn Monroe contrasts sharply with the sexual trashiness of some current female sexual icons.*

seraglio (sə-RAL-yō): a large harem. Derived from Italian *serraglio* (enclosure, cage, harem).

The mansion of Hugh Hefner, creator of Playboy *magazine, has probably sometimes resembled a* **seraglio.**

sergeism (ser-GĀ-izəm): infliction of injury to suppress arousal, based on a story by Tolstoy in which the character of Sergius severs his finger with an ax when his monkish chastity was being threatened by a temptress.

Some members of the suicidal Heaven's Gate cult had themselves castrated, committing **sergeism** *long before they committed suicide.*

sexacmenia (seks-ak-MĒN-ē-ə): that period in people's lives when they achieve the zenith of sexual development or capacity. Derived from Latin *sexus* (sex) and Greek *akmenos* (full grown).

Many men usually achieve their **sexacmenia** *years before women, who often do not fully develop their sexual desires and prowess until at least their thirties.*

sexanhedonia (seks-an-hē-DŌ-nē-ə): loss of one's ability to enjoy sexual acts that formerly gave one pleasure. Derived from Latin *sexus* (sex), Greek *a-* (without), and Greek *hedone* (pleasure).

*Her **sexanhedonia** was a by-product of her generalized inability to experience pleasure of any kind.*

sexautism (seks-Ô-tizəm): the tendency to be preoccupied with sexual thoughts. Derived from Latin *sexus* (sex) and Greek *autos* (self).

*The psychiatrist explained that persons affected by **sexautism** think about sex even more often than most adolescent males.*

sexedonia (seks-ə-DŌN-ə): the thesis or doctrine that complete happiness requires complete satisfaction of the sex urge. Derived from Latin *sexus* (sex) and Greek *hedone* (pleasure).

*Because Hugh believes in **sexedonia**, he thinks that hermits, monks, and celibates cannot possibly be happy.*

sexoclitic (seks-ə-KLIT-ik): tending to express greater sympathy for a member of the opposite sex; said more of men than women. Derived from Latin *sexus* (sex) and Greek *klinein* (to lean).

*Our law professor, Mr. Pound, known for his **sexoclitic** grading, once was overheard remarking that only women are truly civilized.*

sexomentia (seks-ō-MEN-shə, seks-ō-MEN-tē-ə): mental derangement caused by sexual frustration. Derived from Latin *sexus* (sex) and *mens* (mind).

*Tootsie intentionally exacerbated Herbie's **sexomentia** by calling him "crazy" and refusing to sleep with him.*

sexoschizia (seks-ō-SKIZ-ē-ə): either (i) the condition of having bisexual cravings, or (ii) the condition of deriving pleasure from both sadistic and masochistic practices. Derived from Latin *sexus* (sex) and Greek *schizein* (to split).

*Because Mr. Swinburne had **sexoschizia** in both senses of the term, we were not surprised to see him in bed with members of both sexes while receiving and giving pain.*

sexual adiaphoria (SEKS-shōō-əl ad-ē-a-FOR-ē-ə): an incapacity to experience enjoyment from sex, at times coming from overindulgence. Derived from Latin *sexus* (sex) and Greek *adiaphoros* (indifferent).

*So surfeited was Hugh by decades of sexual hedonism that he became subject to **sexual adiaphoria**.*

sexual audility (SEKS-shōō-əl ô-DIL-i-tē): the tendency to be most easily impressed by sexual matters one can hear, such as sexual jokes or anecdotes. Derived from Latin *sexus* (sex) and *audio* (to hear).

*Because of George's **sexual audility**, Jane, his wife, would audiotape their most boisterous sexual bouts to play back later to help induce romance.*

sexual camnosis (SEKS-shōō-əl kam-NŌ-sis): extreme fatigue after intercourse. Derived from Latin *sexus* (sex) and Greek *kamno* (to be exhausted).

*The man was so physically unfit that any sexual bout would lead to a **sexual camnosis** from which he would need at least a week to recover.*

sexual cheromania (SEKS-shōō-əl kerō-MĀN-ē-ə): unusual exaltation and cheerfulness sometimes observed in sexually excited women. Derived from Latin *sexus* (sex) and Greek *chairein* (to rejoice).

*Stella's **sexual cheromania** was infectious, stimulating her lovers to exuberance.*

sexual eburnation (SEKS-shōō-əl ebər-NĀ-shən): an erection of either the penis or the clitoris. Derived from Latin *sexus* (sex) and *eburnus* (of ivory), suggesting hardness.

*When girls would kiss Robert in public, he would be embarrassed by the consequent **sexual eburnation**.*

sexual hegemon (SEKS-shōō-əl HEJ-ə-män): the person showing sexual leadership in a male-female relationship, as in determining the frequency, duration, and mode of intercourse. Derived from Latin *sexus* (sex) and Greek *hegemon* (guide, leader).

*The sexologist was insisting that there is nothing wrong with a woman's being the **sexual hegemon**, since either sex is equally capable of sexual leadership.*

sexual kalopsia (SEKS-shōō-əl ka-LOP/LŌP-sē-ə): heightened sexual interest or desire causing one's female sexual partner to appear much more beautiful than she is. Derived from Latin *sexus* (sex), *kalos* (beautiful) and Greek *ops* (eye).

*His love of his plain-looking wife produced in him a **sexual kalopsia** in which his wife appeared to be a Miss America.*

sexual melancholia (SEKS-shōō-əl mel-ən-KŌ-lē-ə): an obsolete term for "depression caused by a man's belief that he is becoming impotent." *Gerald's wife didn't exactly bolster his ego when she told him that his* *sexual melancholia* was a big concern over something small and insignificant.

sexual nepenthia (SEKS-sh$\overline{oo}$-əl ni/nə-PEN-thē-ə): the use of sex to escape from negative emotions, such as anxiety and depression. Derived from Latin *sexus* (sex) and Greek *nepenthes* (removing sorrow).

*There are people who enjoy sex more highly than most other people, but there are also people who feel driven to sex, not from a sense of joy, but as an escape from negative emotions, as a **sexual nepenthia**.*

sexual ochlesis (SEKS-sh$\overline{oo}$-əl ok-LĒ-sis): a loss of sex drive because of lack of privacy, as in a crowded house or apartment. Derived from Latin *sexus* (sex) and Greek *ochlos* (crowd).

*When Pam moved from a crowded dormitory to her own private apartment, she no longer suffered from **sexual ochlesis** and was able freely to express her passions.*

shrimping: slang term for sucking one's partner's toes.

*Nathan had a foot fetish and liked to tout **shrimping** as safe sex.*

siderodromophilia (sī-dēr-ə-dromə-FIL-ē-ə): sexual arousal from trains. Derived from Greek *siderodromo* (trains) and *philia* (attachment, attraction).

*John and Mary enjoyed indulging their **siderodromophilia** by reserving a train cabin and having sex while standing in front of the window.*

sitophilia (sī-tə-FIL-ē-ə): arousal from using food for sexual purposes, as distinguished from "sitomania," which means "an abnormal craving for food." Many people enjoy using food in sex play and sex games, as when some women use squash, cucumbers, bananas, or sausages in masturbation. More than one man has taken a plum, slit it slightly, pushed it onto the head of his penis, and then inserted his fruit-bearing phallus into his partner's vagina, supposedly to add volume and pressure. Whipped cream and other foods have also been used in sex. Derived from Greek *sitos* (grain, food) and *philia* (attachment, attraction).

*We did not learn about Merwin's **sitophilia** until we caught him in the kitchen as he was pulling a hard-boiled egg out of his rectum.*

smegma (SMEG-mə): a secretion of sebaceous glands that, when it accumulates under the foreskin of the head of the penis or around the labia minora, becomes whitish, cheesy, and smelly.

*When Marty told his blind date that the pudding she had made tasted like **smegma**, he wasn't exactly off to a good start.*

sororilagnia (sə-ror-i-LAG-nē-ə): sexual desire of a brother for his sister. Derived from Latin *soror* (sister) and Greek *lagneia* (lust).

Because brothers and sisters are often together without adult supervision, sororilagnia can develop and lead to actions that parents may not ever discover, or may not discover until years later.

spanecronia (span-ə-KRŌ-nē-ə): condition defined by the meagerness of the seminal fluid in an ejaculation. Derived from Greek *spanos* (scarce) and *ecron* (seminal fluid).

Because Harden would sometimes masturbate several times a day, he would sometimes experience spanecronia.

spaneria (spə-NĀR-ē-ə): scarcity of men, as in certain parts of the world. Derived from Greek *spanos* (scarce) and *aner* (man).

Wars, stress-related diseases, propensities to take risks, and many other factors might explain the spaneria of a particular region of the world.

spectrophilia (spek-trə-FIL-ē-ə): a morbid attraction to, or obsession with, ghosts or spirits, often including the illusion of having sex with spirits. Derived from Latin *spectrum* (appearance, specter, from *specere*, to look) and Greek *philia* (attachment, attraction).

When Betty told Barney that she was sexually assaulted by some spirit, he told her that her spectrophilia was medieval and far too modern for him.

sphallolalia (sfalō-LĀL-ē-ə): erotic talk that is not followed by sex, as in flirtatious badinage. Derived from Greek *sphallo* (to baffle or disappoint) and *latein* (to babble or talk).

The young school athletes were frustrated and angered by the sphallolalia of some of the cheerleaders who would enjoy sexually teasing them.

spheroplania (sferō-PLAN/PLĀN-ē-ə): the flattening of the buttocks, as when some people grow older. Derived from Greek *sphairomata* (buttocks) and Latin *planus* (flat).

As men age they often simultaneously develop spheroplania and swollen stomachs.

stasivalent (stas-i-VĀL-ənt): potent only when standing. Derived from the Greek *stasis* (a standing) and Latin *valere* (to be strong).

When the stasivalent marathon runner said that he has to have sex on the run, we did not realize that he was speaking literally.

stasophallist (stas-ə-FAL-ist): a male who prefers to have intercourse standing. Derived from Greek *stasimos* (standing) and *phallos* (penis).
*Luke was a **stasophallist** who did not have enough time to lie down for sex.*

steatofemoral (stē-*at*-ō-FEM-ər-əl): having fat thighs. Derived from Greek *stear* (fat) and Latin *femur* (thigh).
*Melissa used to be **steatofemoral** until she regularly used her treadmill.*

steatopygia (stē-*at*-ə-PIJ-ē-ə, stē-*at*-PĪ-jē-ə): the condition of having fat buttocks. Derived from Greek *stear* (fat) and *pyge* (buttocks).
*Some men prefer women with **steatopygia** because they believe that they have more flesh to pinch.*

steatopygous (stē-*at*-ə-PĪ-gəs): having fat buttocks. Derived from Greek *stear* (fat) and *pyge* (buttocks).
*When men call most sex hot lines, they will probably never encounter a woman who calls herself "Bertha," precisely because of the popular belief that "Bertha" sounds as if it belongs to a **steatopygous** woman.*

steatosural (stē-*at*-ō-SOOR-əl): having fat leg calves. Derived from Greek *stear* (fat) and Latin *sura* (calf).
*Although some people believe that Robin is **steatosural**, she has muscular calves.*

sthenolagnia (sthenə/ō-LAG-nē-ə): sexual arousal from watching displays of strength. Derived from Greek *sthenos* (strength) and *lagneia* (lust).
*Robert's wife, Carol, was a weightlifting groupie whose **sthenolagnia** moved her to infidelity.*

Stockholm syndrome: the emotional bonding and psychological dependence that can develop between captor and captive, terrorist and hostage, or molester and person molested. Derived from circumstances attendant on a bank robbery in Stockholm, Sweden, in which a female hostage became so emotionally attached to one of the robbers that she broke off an engagement and remained faithful to her former captor during his prison term.
*The psychiatrist speculated that, should the hostages be held for a few more weeks, at least some of them could easily develop attachments associated with the **Stockholm syndrome**.*

strangulation, penile: the interruption of blood circulation in the penis, as when the penis is inserted through a tight metal ring, and swells so much as to prevent removal of the ring. Penile strangulation occurs principally in adolescent males engaged in sexual experimentation. Unless the ring is quickly removed, the penis can develop gangrene.

*Parkin assured us that he won't ever suffer from **penile strangulation** because he always carries a hacksaw during those sexual activities that could most likely lead to that result.*

stuprator (STŌO-prā-tor): a defiler of virgins. Derived from Latin *strupro* (to defile).

*Some **stuprators** are proud of taking away women's virginity.*

succubamania (*suk*-ū-bə-MĀN-ē-ə): a woman's obsessive desire to lie under a man. Derived from Latin *succubare* (to lie under) and Greek *mania* (madness, craving).

*Because of Mary's **succubamania**, her mother called her "mattress girl."*

succubovalent (*suk*-ū-bō-VĀL-ənt): able to perform sexual intercourse only when lying under rather than atop a woman. Derived from Latin *succubare* (to lie under) and *valere* (to be strong).

*The **succubovalent** man insisted that his sexual technique not only gave his wife more freedom of movement but also gave him more energy during intercourse.*

succubus (SUK-yə-bəs): a medieval term for a demon that assumes the shape of a woman, and has sex with a sleeping man. Derived from Latin *succuba* (prostitute, from *succubare*, to lie under).

*Instead of admitting that he would occasionally experience "wet dreams," Goober would insist that he was overcome by a **succubus**.*

supinovalent (sōō-pī-nō-VĀL-ənt): potent sexually and capable of intercourse only in the face-up position. Derived from Latin *supinus* (lying on the back) and *valere* (to be strong).

*Because Ted was **supinovalent**, he would always be on his back during intercourse.*

suraphilous (sōō-RAF-ə-ləs): especially attracted to calves. Derived from Latin *sura* (calf) and *philein* (to love).

*Because Herman was **suraphilous**, he asked his girlfriend, Sally, always to wear dresses and never to wear slacks.*

symbolic masturbation: the theoretical idea that certain repetitive acts, such as twisting a strand of hair, stroking or rubbing one's nose, or pulling one's earlobes are substitutes for masturbation.

*Buster was stroking his nose with such enthusiasm during the porn movie that Chelsea accused him of **symbolic masturbation**.*

symphorophilia (sim-for-ə-FIL-ē-ə): a term coined by *Lovemaps* author John Money to refer to sexual arousal from creating casualties, as from burning down or bombing buildings with people in them. Whether harming others gives some people a feeling of power over others, or satisfies other desires that have sexual associations, some people describe the satisfaction achieved by destroying others in sexual language. Derived from Greek *symthoma* (casualty), *phoron* (producer), and *philia* (attachment, attraction).

*While many people are disgusted by harm done by **symphorophilia**, some of them find the eroticization of violence, as in the movie* Body Double, *entertaining.*

synorgasmia (sin-or-GAZ-mē-ə): simultaneous orgasms in both partners. Derived from Greek *syn* (with, together with, at the same time) and *orgasmos* (a swelling).

*While **synorgasmia** is great when it happens, it is unrealistic and foolish for sexual partners to expect it to occur all or even most of the time.*

syntribadism (sin-TRIB-ə-dizəm): female masturbation in which the legs are crossed, and the thighs are rubbed against each other. Derived from Greek *syn* (together) and *tribein* (to rub).

*Bunny told Vince that because she, as a teenager, had mastered the art of **syntribadism**, she can masturbate without the use of probes and other artificial aids.*

T

tachorgasmia (tak-or-GAZ-mē-ə): the reaching of orgasm in a shorter than normal time, especially in the male. Derived from Greek *tachos* (speed) and *organ* (to swell).

*Norbert's **tachorgasmia** was so serious that he ejaculated before he even penetrated Matilda.*

tachyorthosis (*tak*-ē-or-THŌ-sis): the capacity to achieve an erection quickly. Derived from Greek *tachys* (fast) and *orthosis* (the condition of being erect or straight).

*Healthy, young males often pride themselves on their **tachyorthosis**, which enables them to perform sexually at a moment's notice.*

tactus (TAK-tus): a skillful lover's graceful and delicate touch, usually referring to the hands but also applicable to the touch of the lips, sex organs, and other parts of the body. Derived from Latin *tactus* (past participle of *tangere* [to touch]).

    *Florence complimented Warren, her most gentle lover, on his **tactus**.*

talophilous (tə-LOF-i-ləs): especially attracted to female ankles. Derived from Latin *talus* (ankle) and Greek *philein* (to love).

    *Francis was so **talophilous** that he could not resist licking Zelda's ankles.*

tantaleuse (TAN-tə-LO͞OS/Lə(R)Z): a female who tries to excite a man's sexual appetites without any intention to satisfy them, described in vulgar slang as a "cockteaser." Derived from the mythological Greek king Tantalos, who was punished for divulging the secrets of the gods to mortals by having forever out of his reach water and food (fruit).

    *The sexual teasing by a **tantaleuse** can anger and even enrage men, especially when they misinterpret the teasing as representing a strong desire for action.*

tantalolagnia (tantə-lə-LAG-nē-ə): a condition in which a male can be aroused enough for intercourse only from being sexually teased. Derived from the Greek king Tantalos (*see entry above*) and Greek *lagneia* (lust).

    *Michelle's desire to satisfy her boyfriend's **tantalolagnia** led her to tease him for at least thirty minutes before they would have sex.*

taphephilia (taf-ə-FIL-ē-ə): sexual arousal from being buried alive. Derived from Greek *taphe* (burial) and *philia* (attachment, attraction).

    *In asking Judy and Elroy to mummify him in rubber and then bury him, George revealed his **taphephilia**.*

tardojacia (tar-dō-JAS/JĀS-ē-ə): the ability of a male to withhold his ejaculation during intercourse, especially to allow the woman to have an orgasm. Derived from Latin *tardus* (slow) and *eiaculari* (to throw out).

    ***Tardojacia** is an essential attribute for any male porn star, since most viewers don't want to see the ending of a movie shortly after the opening credits.*

tardorgasmus (tar-dor-GAZ-mus): an orgasm attained only after much effort at coitus, as when one or both parties have overindulged, or are not enjoying the experience, or have sexual organs that do not fit together well. Derived from Latin *tardus* (slow) and Greek *orgasmos* (swelling).

    *Hank's **tardorgasmus** was so slow in arriving that his wife had fallen asleep.*

tautaner (TÔ-tan-ur): a male homosexual. Derived from Greek *to auto* (the same) and *aner* (man).

*Whenever a man is the least bit effeminate, many people will assume— sometimes incorrectly—that he is a **tautaner**.*

telephone scatalogia (TEL-ə-fōn ska-tə-LOJ/LŌJ-ē-ə): exhibitionism in which a person achieves sexual arousal from talking on the phone about sexual matters to unknown listeners—in short, making obscene phone calls. Derived from Greek *skato-* (dung) and *logos* (word, reason, speech).

*Quinby's boss warned her against telephone **scatalogia**, telling her that such activity should be engaged in only when she is off the clock.*

tempasthentic (tem-pas-THEN-tik): losing sexual vitality or energy as times goes on. Derived from Latin *tempus* (time), Greek *a-* (without), and Greek *sthenos* (strength).

*We wondered how a **tempasthentic** eighty-five-year-old could hope to satisfy a vigorous twenty-five-year-old woman.*

temuvalent (tem-ū-VĀL-ənt): able to have sexual intercourse only under the influence of alcohol. Derived from Latin *temulentus* (drunken) and *valere* (to be strong).

***Temuvalent** people can have sex only in an impaired state.*

teratophallia (terə-tə-FAL-ē-ə): deformity of the penis. Derived from Greek *teras* (monster) and *phallos* (penis).

*Because the other boys would make fun of Shamus's **teratophallia**, he would often go to a far-off corner of the locker room to change his clothes.*

thalpotentiginy (thal-pō-ten-TIJ-ə-nē): sexual arousal produced by warmth, including warm weather. Derived from Greek *thalpos* (warmth) and Latin *tentigo* (lust, passion).

*His **thalpotentiginy** was so strong that women would avoid approaching him when he was under a sun lamp.*

thelelingus (thelə-LING-gəs): the erotic licking of the female nipples. Derived from Greek *thele* (nipple) and Latin *lingere* (to lick).

*Because nipples are a highly sensitive erogenous zone, and because most men like female breasts, men who perform **thelelingus** are usually in a win-win situation.*

thelemassation (thelə-ma-SĀ-shən): the erotic fingering of the nipples. Derived from Greek *thele* (nipple) and *massein* (to knead).

*Because of Brad's digital skill, his **thelemassation** delighted Allison.*

thelerethism (thelə-RETH-izəm): erection of the nipple from stimulation, as in foreplay. Derived from Greek *thele* (nipple) and *erethisma* (a stirring).
> *Our friend Christopher, a connoisseur of porn, says that one sign of female stimulation is **thelerethism**.*

thelorthia (thə-LOR-thēə): the erection of one or both nipples. Derived from Greek *thele* (nipple) and *orthosis* (straightening).
> *Belinda's **thelorthia** was a good indicator of her sexual excitement.*

thelyflorescence (thelə-flô-RES-əns): the flowering of feminine characteristics in a young girl. Derived from Greek *thlys* (female) and Latin *florere* (to bloom).
> *In beauty pageants of young girls, mothers will often use makeup and clothes to accentuate the girls' **thelyflorescence**.*

thelymania (thel-i-MĀN-ē-ə): an obsolete term for excessive and uncontrollable male lust or **satyriasis** *(see entry)*. Derived from the Greek *thelys* (female) and *mania* (madness, craving).
> *Some politicians ruin their careers because of their **thelymania**.*

thelyphthoric (thel-ip-THOR-ik): pertaining to what corrupts women. Derived from the Greek *thelys* (female) and *-phthora* (destruction, death, corruption).
> *In the movie* Carrie, *the mother of the title character was constantly concerned to protect her daughter from **thelyphthoric** influences.*

thesauromania (thi-sôrō-MĀN-ē-ə): compulsion to collect objects or clothing belonging to women. Derived from Greek *thesaurus* (treasure) and *mania* (madness, craving).
> *Melvin tried to conceal his **thesauromania**, but was unsuccessful when his sister found all her missing panties in his closet.*

thigmosis (thig-MŌ-sis): a compulsion to touch things, especially a woman's private parts. Derived from Greek *thigma* (touch) and *-osis* (an abnormal condition).
> *The manager of the strip club warned his customers against indulging their **thigmosis**, especially during lap dances.*

thygatria (thi-GAT-rē-ə): sexual intercourse with one's own daughter. Derived from *thygater* (daughter).
> *Although Bill Clinton has had sex with at least one person who was at the time close to his daughter's age, there is no evidence that he has ever engaged in **thygatria**.*

thygatrilagnia (thi-gat-ri-LAG-nē-ə): sexual desire of a father for his daughter. Derived from Greek *thygater* (daughter) and *lagneia* (lust).
Although the TV character of Archie Bunker clearly loved his daughter Gloria, it is clear that the love was quite nonsexual and not **thygatrilagnia**.

tibialoconcupiscent (tibi-al-ō-kon-KU-pi-sənt): tending to enjoy watching a female put on her hose or stockings. Derived from Latin *tibiale* (stocking, legging) and *concupiscentia* (strong or ardent desire).
The man bought his wife sexy hosiery so that he could indulge his **tibialoconcupiscent** *fantasies.*

timophilia (tim-ō-FIL-ē-ə): sexual arousal from wealth. Derived from Greek *time* (value, worth) and *philia* (attachment, attraction).
Known for his lust, the Roman emperor Caligula would sometimes also display **timophilia**, *as when he wallowed in piles of gold.*

timotrudia (timō-TROO-dē-ə): sexual timidity, especially in men, as when they are bashful in approaching women or performing sexual intercourse. Derived from Greek *timor* (anxiety or apprehension) and Latin *intrudere* (to thrust into).
Some men need, or at least think that they need, liquor to overcome their **timotrudia**, *which can paralyze them in their sexual relations.*

tithiolagnia (tith-ē-ō-LAG-nē-ə): arousal from nursing. Derived from the Greek *titheneo* (to nurse) and *lagneia* (lust).
While John's wife found nursing her baby pleasant, we would not go so far as to say that she was affected by **tithiolagnia**.

tithioscopia (tith-ē-ō-SKŌP-ē-ə): observing with sexual desire a nursing woman, or the depiction of a nursing woman (as in an illustration). Derived from Greek *titheneo* (to nurse) and *skopein* (to observe).
When Milford, an archopponent of feminism, insisted that anyone opposed to public breastfeeding is a prude, we suspected him of **tithioscopia**.

tragolimia (trag-ō-LIM/LĒM-ē-ə): compulsion in males to have sex, regardless of the attractiveness of the partner; **satyriasis** (*see entry*) in which the male desires sex with *any* woman, regardless of her age, physical appearance, and any other attributes. Derived from Greek *tragos* (he-goat) and *limos* (hunger). For centuries the goat has been a symbol for lechery and licentiousness.
When the representative was caught in bed with three brownies, four

*female rap artists, and five members of Hadassah, his **tragolimia** was exposed.*

tribade (TRIB-əd): lesbian. From the Greek *tribein* (to rub).
*While male homosexuality is often the object of negative comments, **tribades** are often considered sexy and fashionable.*

tribadism (TRIB-ə-dizəm): lesbianism. From the Greek *tribein* (to rub).
*One navy officer during the Second World War told General Eisenhower that **tribadism** was so common in the navy that to remove it effectively would require discharging all women from the navy.*

trichophilia (trik-ō-FIL-ē-ə): sexual arousal from hair, as when people view, touch, cut, or collect it. Derived from Greek *thrix* (hair) and *philia* (attachment to, attraction).
*In the 1980s in the Alderman Library at the University of Virginia, rumor has it that a person affected by **trichophilia** would snip locks of sleeping women's hair.*

troilism (TROI-lizəm): a triadic or triangular relationship in which a man has sexual relations with a woman, and then watches her have relations with another woman or a man. Similarly, a woman may have sex with a man, and then watch him have sex with another person. Derived from Latin *tria* (three).
*Because Mildred was worried that her son Fox would engage in **troilism**, she never permitted him to have more than one visitor at a time in his bedroom.*

turpicunnia (tur-pi-KUN-ē-ə): the condition of having an unattractive or ugly vulva, such as one in which the labia majora are thin and flaccid instead of plump and firm, or one in which the vaginal entrance is gaping or surrounded by scar tissue. Derived from Latin *turpis* (vile, foul) and *cunnus* (vulva, female external genitalia).
*When Howard made fun of Allison's **turpicunnia** in public, onlookers predicted that their relationship could soon end.*

U

ultimate kiss: a colloquial term for "deep-throat" fellatio.
*Because of Monica Lewinsky's **ultimate kiss**, many Republicans and*

several comedians would sometimes refer to the "Oval Office" as the "Oral Office."

undinism (UN-dēn-izəm): a term for an erotic interest in urine, as in **urolagnia** (*see entry*). Derived from the name of a Franco-Germanic female water sprite, Undine or Ondine.

*While we knew Louie collected and tested urine specimens, we did not suspect him of **undinism** until we saw him sniffing urinals.*

uniparous (ū-NIP-ə-rəs): pertaining to a woman who has given birth only one time. The term can also describe a delivery resulting in only one baby. Derived from Latin *unus* (one) and *parere* (to give birth).

*When Kelly was asked whether she wanted to have another child, she responded that she wanted to remain **uniparous**.*

univaleur (ū-ni-və-LUR): a man who can perform sexual intercourse only once at a given time, as during one night. Derived from Latin *unus* (one) and *valere* (to be strong).

*Ralph told Wendy that, since she knew that he was a **univaleur** when they got married, she should not pester him for two sexual bouts in one night.*

unpleasure: a psychoanalytic term for the tension, pain, and frustration people feel when the pleasure drive of the id is denied, as when people do not satisfy their desires for sex and food.

*When Jane would not accede to Dick's sexual requests, Dick told her that his consequent **unpleasure** could cause both of them much grief.*

uranism (YOOR-nizəm): an obsolete term for "male homosexuality," coined by Karl Henrich Ulrichs in 1862 and derived from Aphrodite Urania, the Greek goddess of heavenly love.

*In the United States, lesbianism is less controversial than **uranism**.*

uranist (YOORə-nist): an obsolete term for a "male homosexual." Derived from Aphrodite. Urania, the Greek goddess of heavenly love.

*The one hundred-year-old psychoanalyst referred to Michelangelo as a **uranist**.*

urinism (YUR-in-izəm): sexual activity in which urine or urination figures. Derived from the Latin word *urina* (urine).

*We had no idea what Theodore and Edith were talking about when they said that they were expecting "golden showers" until we discovered that their sexual practices included **urinism**.*

urning (ŏŏrning): a male homosexual. Derived from Greek irregular form of Urania, the love goddess Aphrodite.
*Many heterosexual women prefer the company of **urnings** to that of heterosexual men because the women feel that they need not worry about sexual exploitation.*

urolagnia (yōōrō-LAG-nē-ə): attraction to, or arousal from, the urine or the urinary processes of one's sexual partner or others. Derived from Latin *urina* (urine) and Greek *lagneia* (lust).
*We did not realize that Hannibal and Clarice were interested in **urolagnia** until we saw the rubber sheet on their bed.*

urolagniac (yōōrō-LAG-nē-ak): a person who derives sexual pleasure from urine or urination. Derived from Latin *urina* (urine), Greek *lagneia* (lust).
*A confirmed **urolagniac**, Chester would encourage his wife to relieve herself on him while the two were in the bathtub.*

uxoravalent (uk-sorō-VĀL-ənt): able to have sex with only someone other than one's wife. Derived from the Latin *uxor* (wife) and *valere* (to be strong).
*The evangelist condemned the **uxoravalent** playboy.*

uxoriosis (uk-sor-ē-Ō-sis): masochistic submission to one's wife. Derived from Latin *uxor* (wife) and Greek *-osis* (state, process, condition).
*Women who are much stronger in several ways than their husbands can promote **uxoriosis** in their marriage.*

uxorious (uk-SOR-ē-əs): characterized by excessively doting on, and showing an excessive submission to, one's wife. Derived from Latin *uxor* (wife).
Jim Backus, in Rebel Without A Cause, *played the role of a timid, **uxorious** husband.*

uxorodespotism (uk-sorō-DES-pə-*tiz*-əm): excessive domination by a wife. Derived from Latin *uxor* (wife) and English *despotism*.
*When Brunhilda locked her husband in his room until he made his bed, she was revealing a glimpse of the **uxorodespotism** that ruined their marriage.*

uxoromania (uk-sorə-MĀN-ē-ə): excessive sexual craving for one's wife. Derived from Latin *uxor* (wife) and Greek *mania* (madness, strong urge).
*So strong was Zeke's **uxoromania** that he could not be with his wife more than one minute without hugging, kissing, and fondling her.*

uxoromatria (uk-sorō-MAT/MĀT-rē-ə): the mindset of a man who wants his spouse to have the spirit and demeanor of both a wife and a mother. Derived from the Latin *uxor* (wife) and *mater* (mother).

*Lefty's wife, a psychiatrist, said that his **uxoromatria** stemmed from his never having resolved his Oedipus complex.*

uxoronequent (uk-sorə-NEK-kwənt): unable to perform sexual intercourse with one's own wife because of the absence of attraction. Derived from Latin *uxor* (wife) and *nequeo* (to be unable).

*Instead of taking responsibility for his marital infidelities, the rock star held that his wife's disregard for her appearance led to his **uxoronequent** condition and his trysts.*

uxorosthen (uk-sor-ROS-thɛn): a male potent only with his wife. Derived from Latin *uxor* (wife) and Greek *sthenos* (strong).

*Al was described as a contented **uxorosthen**, whose wife was sufficient for his needs.*

V

vaginismus (VAJ-ə-*niz*-məs): a painful spasmodic contraction of the vagina. Derived from Latin *vagina* (vagina, scabbard) and *-ismus* (suffix designating a state or condition).

*After intercourse, Sarah experienced **vaginismus**, and was in no mood to talk.*

vaginoraptus (vaj-i-nō-RAP-təs): sexual intercourse with one's wife against her will. Derived from Latin *vagina* (vagina, scabbard) and *rapere* (to seize).

*Unfortunately, there are still a number of states where **vaginoraptus** does not qualify as rape, since the wife is thought of as the property of the husband.*

varietist (və-RĪ-i-tist): one who practices unconventional sex. Derived from the idea of variation or difference.

*An overt **varietist** in Hollywood is treated differently from an overt varietist in, say, Pocatello, Idaho.*

venery (VEN-ə-rē): sexual intercourse; pursuit of indulgence in sexual pleasures. Derived from Middle English *venerie*, from Old French, from Medieval Latin *veneria*, from Latin *venus* (desire, love).

*Acts of **venery** should not be broadcast on regular commercial television.*

ventustulimia (ven-*tōōs*-tə-LIM/LĒM-ē-ə): a strong desire to be beautiful and sexually attractive. Derived from Latin *venustus* (charming, lovely) and Greek *limos* (hunger, famine).
> *Beauty and fashion magazines cater to not only people who enjoy beauty but also people who have **ventustulimia**.*

vernorexia (vur-nə-REK-sē-ə): the increase in romantic desire in the spring. Derived from Latin *ver* (spring) and Latin/Greek *orexis* (appetite).
> *Because it was April, we fully expected young people to indulge their **vernorexia**.*

vertergate (VUR-tər-gāt): to turn back or around and look at a passerby. Derived from Latin *verto* (to turn) and *tergum* (back).
> *After he **vertergated**, he ogled the young woman.*

vincilagnia (vin-si-LAG-nē-ə): arousal from bondage. Derived from Latin *vinco* (to conquer) and Greek *lagneia* (lust).
> *When Herman told us that Lily was all tied up, we had no idea that he was alluding to **vincilagnia**.*

viraginity (virə-JIN-i-te): a condition of a woman with physical characteristics associated with men. Derived from Latin *virago* (female warrior, from *vir*, man).
> *Robin's deep voice, extremely short hair, muscular body, and sexually ambiguous name all contributed to her **viraginity**.*

virago (və-RÄ-gō): an old term for an ill-tempered, shrewish woman.
> *An actress can appear to be sensitive and genteel on screen, and yet be a **virago** off screen.*

virgynation (vēr-ji-NĀ-shən): sexual intercourse between husband and wife. Derived from Latin *vir* (man) and Greek *gyn-* (woman).
> *Even **virgynation** can be illegal in the Commonwealth of Virginia if the man and wife do not adopt the prescribed sexual positions.*

virilescence (*vēr*-i-LES-əns): the gradual appearance of masculine characteristics in women, such as facial hair and deeper voice, especially after menopause. Derived from Latin *vir* (adult male) and *-escence* (noun suffix meaning "becoming").
> *Although we knew about **virilescence**, we were surprised to see Sheldon's mom sporting a full beard and singing bass.*

virilingus (*vēr*-i-LING-gəs): the erotic licking of the male sex organs. Derived from Latin *virilia* (male sex organs) and *lingere* (to lick).

*Although there was a time in the United States when most people called oral sex "perverted," oral sex, including **virilingus**, is widely practiced in America today.*

virilism (VĒR-ə-*liz*-əm): development of male secondary sexual characteristics in a woman. Derived from Latin *vir* (man).

*Ida's **virilism** was hardly noticeable—until she developed a mustache and won the "Mr. Idaho" bodybuilding contest.*

volutate (VOL-ū-tāt): to have sexual intercourse with a woman having a spacious vagina. Derived from Latin *voluto* (to roll).

*The smart-alecky adolescent asserted that **volutating** is the best exercise one can get while lying down.*

voyeur (voi-YUR, vwo-YUR): a person whose sexual desire is focused on seeing sex organs and sexual acts. Derived from French for "one who sees," from *voir* (to see).

*A **voyeur** can often indulge his desires without appearing at all odd, as when he goes to a "gentlemen's club."*

vulvolimia (vul-və-LIM/LĒM-ē-ə): insatiable desire for the external genitalia of females. Derived from Latin *vulva* (covering, womb) and Greek *limos* (hunger).

*Jerry's **vulvolimia** so dominated his life that he had trouble concentrating unless he had sex with some female at least every other day.*

W

water sports: slang term referring to sexual arousal from urine and urination, often abbreviated as "w/s" in personal ads.

*We thought that Tewey's interest in **water sports** meant that he enjoyed such activities as sailing and skiing, not that he enjoyed drinking three six-packs of beer with his wife and friends and playing "Who's my toilet?"*

whoreson: an old-fashioned and Shakespearean insult accusing a man of being the son of a prostitute.

*The wealthy pimp used to brag that he began life as a humble **whoreson** and rose, through unremitting hard work and entrepreneurial skill, to the enviable heights of a "flesh-merchant."*

wittol (WIT-l): an archaic word for a man who is aware of, and submits to, his wife's infidelity. Derived from medieval English *wetewold* (from *weten*, *witen* to be aware, to know and *-wold*).

> *Because Frank enjoyed the benefits of having a wealthy wife, we were not surprised that he didn't mind being a **wittol**.*

working girl: a euphemism for "prostitute."

> *We had no idea that Jackie was a **working girl** until we saw her peddling her flesh in a seedy part of downtown.*

wrong door: a slang term for the anus, used in talk of anal sex.

> *The porn star insisted that she did not enjoy sex through the **wrong door**, even though it poses much less of a risk of pregnancy than sex through the more usual entrance.*

X

xenodynamic (*zen*-ə-dī-NAM-ik): sexually potent with unfamiliar females but impotent with one's wife. Derived from Greek *xenos* (stranger) and *dynamis* (power).

> *Although familiarity breeds contempt, **xenodynamic** persons should not feel free to have sex with persons other than their spouses.*

xenolytria (zen-ə-LĬT-rē-ə): sexual infidelity by a married man. Derived from Greek *xenos* (stranger) and *elytron* (cover, sheath, shell).

> *The mayor's **xenolytria** was well known, since he would often be seen with his lover in public.*

xenophallia (zen-ə-FAL-ē-ə): sexual infidelity by a married woman. Derived from Greek *xenos* (stranger) and *phallos* (penis).

> *The proverbial pool boy tempted Querida to commit **xenophallia**.*

xerotripsis (zērə-TRIP-sis): intercourse ending without ejaculation. Derived from Greek *xeros* (dry) and *tripsis* (friction).

> *After Michael's **xerotripsis** he said that he was dry at the pump.*

Y

yard: an old euphemism for the penis.

> *The porn star claimed that his **yard** was one-third yard long.*

yehudi (yǝ-HOO-dē): slang for a Jewish penis. Derived from the connection to an obviously Jewish-sounding name.
*Rosalind preferred Jewish men because she preferred a **yehudi** to an uncircumcised phallus.*

yoni (YŌNĒ): the Hindu name for the vagina worshiped in Tantric rites throughout India. It is depicted in a figure, and serves as the formal symbol under which Shakti, the dynamic energy of a Hindu god (such as Sira), is worshiped.
*When the fun-loving fraternity learned about **yoni** in his class on world religions, he said that he too worships **yoni**, after a manner.*

Z

zelophilia (zelǝ-FIL-ē-ǝ): attraction to, or arousal from, jealousy, triggered by the jealousy of either partner. Derived from Greek *zelos* (zeal) and *philia* (attachment, attraction).
*Because Merlin was given to **zelophilia**, he would take his adventurous wife to an orgy just so that he could experience an adrenaline rush caused by his jealousy over his wife's having sex with other men.*

zooerasty (zoǝ-Ē-rastē): sexual arousal or gratification from contact with an animal. Derived from the Greek *zoon* (animal) and *erastes* (lover). Also called **zoophilia** (*see entry*).
*During Egbert's enlistment in the marines, he was asked whether he had ever experienced **zooerasty**.*

zoolagnia (zōǝ-LAG-nē-ǝ): sexual arousal from contact with animals. Derived from the Greek *zoon* (animal) and *lagneia* (lust).
In Woody Allen's movie Everything You Always Wanted to Know About Sex (But Were Afraid to Ask), *the actor Gene Wilder plays a character who enjoys **zoolagnia** with a sheep.*

zoophilia (zōǝ-FIL-ē-ǝ): attachment and attraction to farm animals or household pets in preference to human beings. Derived from the Greek *zoon* (animal) and *philia* (attachment, attraction).
*The former Midwestern senator—and former farmboy—could not understand why indignation at his **zoophilia** extended beyond animal rights groups.*

zoosadist (zoǝ-SĀ-dist): a person who derives sexual pleasure from injuring animals. Derived from Greek *zoon* (animal) and *sadist* (from the Parisian aristocrat Marquis de Sade, known for his sexually abusive practices).

> *The* National Lampoon *magazine once had a cartoon strip that might have appealed to* **zoosadists**. *It featured animal characters resembling Tom and Jerry, and presented the Jerry character as putting a stick of dynamite into the rectum of the Tom character before blowing up the cat's buttocks.*

Reversicon

The second part of this book consists of a reverse dictionary, in which definitions or descriptions of concepts appear in alphabetical order followed by words fitting the definitions. The reverse dictionary or reversicon consists of the following headings: Attracted to/ Aroused by, Beautiful, Belief That, Breasts, Dung, Homosexual, Irrational Fear of, Kissing, Marriage, Masturbation, Oral Sex, Orgasm (s), Penis(es), Prostitute(s), Sexual Intercourse, Vagina(s), and Virgin(s).

Each heading is followed by a horizontal line and parentheses. Accordingly, the heading for "Irrational Fear of" appears as "Irrational Fear of (___)." Under that heading are definitions, most of which are highly telegraphic, almost like crossword clues. Each definition contains a horizontal line or bar. That line or bar should be read as if it is the name of the heading. For example, under the heading called "Irrational Fear of (___)," you'll find the definition "___ sex," which should read "irrational fear of sex." The word by that definition is "erotophobia," about which you can find more information in the main part of the book.

ATTRACTED TO/AROUSED BY (___)

____ activities and objects appropriate only for children: ANACLITISM
____ adolescent males (said of other males): EPHEBOPHILIA
____ afternoon: DELINOLAGNIA
____ ankles: TALOPHILOUS
____ ants: FORMICOPHILIA
____ anuses: ANOPHILOUS
____ backs of females: NOTOPHILOUS
____ bashfulness in females: AIDOCRATIA
____ beating people with canes: RHABDOLAGNIA
____ bees or bee stings: MELISSOPHILIA
____ being fondled in front of others: GREGOMULCIA
____ being physically swayed: BASCULOPHILIA
____ being raped or robbed: HARPAXOPHILIA
____ being tied up: MERINTHOLAGNIA
____ belief that sex partners have terminal diseases: NOSOPHILIA
____ blinded but not blind sex partners: AMAUROPHILIA
____ bodily secretions: HYGROPHILIA
____ bondage: VINCILAGNIA
____ breasts being sucked or suckled: MYZOEROTICISM
____ brothers: FRATILAGNIA
____ buttocks: GLUTOLATRY, GLUTOMANIA, PYGOPHILOUS
____ buttocks-viewing: DERRIEROSCOPIA
____ calves (of legs): SUROPHILOUS
____ cleavage: HYSILATRY
____ coldness: PSYCHROCISM
____ collecting and displaying "pin-up" girls: GYMNOGRAPHEPHILIA
____ creating casualties: SYMPHOROPHILIA
____ crowds: OCHLOPHILIA
____ dancing: CHOREOPHILIA
____ defecating: CHEZOLAGNIA
____ defilement, filth: AUTOMYSOPHILIA
____ dirt, soiled things: MYSOPHILIA
____ disrobing in front of others: ECYDYOSIS, ECDYSIASM
____ dung: COPROPHILIA
____ elderly men: GERONTOPHILIA
____ enemas: KLISMAPHILIA
____ fantasizing about having sex with someone other than current partner: ALLORGASMIA

____ fantasizing about loss of one's body parts: APOTEMNOPHILIA
____ fantasizing that one is a corpse: AUTONECROPHILIA
____ fantasizing that one's sexual partner is an amputee: ACROTO-
      MOPHILIA
____ farts: EPROCTOPHILIA
____ feet: PODOPHILIA
____ female adolescents: NYMPHOPHILIA
____ female undergarments: CRYPTOVESTIPHILIA
____ figures, statues: GALATEISM
____ fires: PYROLAGNIA
____ genitalia: EDEOMANIA
____ hair: TRICHOPHILIA
____ heights: ACROPHILIA
____ high-heeled women: ALTOCALCIPHILIA
____ humiliation: ASTHENOLAGNIA
____ hurting men: ARSENOSADISM
____ hurting women: GYNESADISM
____ infantile role-playing: AUTONEPIOPHILIA, AUTOPEDOPHILIA
____ infants of the opposite sex: NEPIOLAGNIA
____ intercourse with a person of a different body type from oneself:
      MORPHOPHILIA
____ intercourse with one-legged partners: MONOPEDOMANIA
____ "kneading" a woman's flesh, especially breasts: MALAXOMANIA,
      SARMASSOPHILIA
____ knees: GONYPHILOUS
____ lactating breasts: LACTAPHILIA
____ large genitalia: MACROGENITALISM
____ legs: CNEMOPALMIA, CNEMOTAXIS, CRUROCENTRIC, CRU-
      ROPHILOUS
____ lips: CHEILOPHILOUS, LEGORASTIA
____ lovers known to have committed an outrage: HYBRISTOPHILIA
____ music: MELOLAGNIA
____ nakedness: OMOLAGNIA
____ noses: NASOPHILIA
____ nursing: TITHIOLAGNIA
____ odor of sweat: HIDROPHRODISIA
____ odors, perfume: OLFACTOLAGNIA, OSMOLAGNIA, OSPHRESIO-
      PHILIA
____ old females: ANILILAGNIA
____ one part of body: PARTIALISM

one ____ farts: EPROCTOLAGNIAC, EPROCTOPHILE
one ____ hairy men: HIRSUTOPHILE
one ____ knees: GENUPHILE
one ____ odors: OSPHRESIOLAGNIAC, RENIFLEUR
one ____ opposite sex: HETEROPHILE
one ____ seeing naked women: GYMNOGYNOMANIAC
one ____ unusual sex or sexual stimuli: PARAPHILE
____ peeping through windows: CRYPTOSCOPOPHILIA, PARASCOP-
ISM
____ penises: PHALLOPHILIA
____ performing in public: AUTAGONISTOPHILIA
____ persons fully clothed: ENDYTOLAGNIA
____ physical deformities: DYSMORPHOPHILIA
____ pictures, statues: ICONOLAGY
____ pregnant women: CYESOLAGNIA, MAIEUSIOPHILIA
____ prostitutes: PORNOLAGNIA
____ receiving ear-blowing: DIAPNOLAGNIA
____ rubbing bodies with dancing partners: CHOROTRIPSIS
____ rubbing genitals on strangers in public: FROTTAGE
____ sacred objects: HIEROPHILIA
____ seeing animals have sex: FAUNOIPHILIA, MIXOSCOPIC ZOO-
PHILIA
____ seeing armpits: MASCHALOLAGNIA
____ seeing displays of strength: STHENOLAGNIA
____ seeing men touch women's genitals: ARRHENOTHIGMOPHILOUS
____ seeing one's own body: AUTOSCOPOPHILIA
____ seeing sex through sheer fabrics: DIAPHANOPHILIA
____ seeing women put on hosiery: TIBIALOCONCUPISCENT
____ seeing women's cleavage: HYSILATRY
____ sermons: HOMILOPHILIA
____ sexually assaulting people: BIASTOPHILIA
____ sinning: PECATTIPHILIA
____ sounds: ACOUSTICOPHILIA
____ spiders: ARACHNEPHILIA
____ spirits, ghosts: SPECTROPHILIA
____ stealing: KLEPTOLAGNIA
____ stimulation to any bodily opening: MEATOSTHESIA
____ stomachs: ALVINOLAGNIA
____ tears of women: DACRYLAGNIA
____ teenaged boys (said of men): HEBEPHILIA

____   teeth: ODONTOPHILIA
____   thighs of females: FEMORMIA, MEROPHILOUS
____   tickling others, being tickled: KNISMOLAGNIA
____   touching, being touched: HAPHEMANIA
____   touching certain materials: HYPHEPHILIA
____   touching females: SARMASSOPHILIA
____   touching one's own body: IPSITHIGMOPHILOUS
____   trains: SIDERODROMOPHILIA
____   travel: HODOPHILIA
____   trees: DENDROPHILIA
____   unusual, bizarre sex: EXOPHILIA
____   urine: UROLAGNIA
____   vaginas: AIDOMANIA, VULVOLIMIA
____   vomit: EMETOPHILIA
____   warmth: THALPOTENTIGINY
____   wealth: TIMOPHILIA
____   whipping: MASTIGOTHYMIA, MASTILAGNIA
____   women older than oneself: GERAFAVIC
____   writing love poems or letters: EROTOGRAPHOMANIA
____   young females: BLASTOLAGNIA, NEANILAGNIA

BEAUTIFUL (___)

___ breasts: CALLICOLPOS
delusion that one is ___: CALLOMANIA
female with ___ buttocks: CALLIPYGETTE
female with ___ vagina: CALLITREMA
possessing ___ breasts: CALLIMASTIAN
possessing ___ breasts and buttocks: CALLIMAMMAPYGIAN
possessing ___ buttocks: CALLIPYGIAN
possessing ___ calves (of legs): CALLISURAL
possessing ___ hair: CALLITRICHOUS
___ woman: KALEIDOGYN

BELIEF THAT (___)

____   happiness requires complete sexual fulfillment: SEXEDONIA

____   one's penis is repulsive to women: PHALLOCACOSIS

____   penis size is indicated by foot size: PEDOMENTIA

____   people at birth are undetermined in their sexual appetites and orientations: PANEROTIC POTENTIAL

____   sex colors or determines all behavior: PANSEXUALISM

____   true love is possible only for mature persons: ORASTORGIA

____   true love is possible only for young persons: PAPPOSTORGIA

BREAST(S) (___)

adoration of cleavage of ___: HYPSILATRY
arousal from having ___ sucked or suckled: MYZOEROTICISM
arousal from watching nursing from ___: TITHIOSCOPIA
beautiful ___: CALLICOLPIA, CALLICOLPOS
bobbing of ___: MAMMAQUATIA
erection of nipples of ___: THELORTHIA
erection of nipples of ___ from stimulation: THELERETHISM
fingering nipples of ___: THELEMASSATION
hanging ___: MAZECTENIA
having beautiful ___: CALLIMASTIAN
having deep ___: BATHYCOLPIAN
having large ___: MAMMOSE
"kneading" of ___: MAZMASSATION
lust centered on ___: MAZOCENTRIC
manipulation of ___: PECTOTAGE
nipple of ___: MAMILLA
obsessive thoughts about ___: MASTOPHRENIA
ogling of ___: MAMMASKEPSIS
one breast larger than the other ___: ANISOMASTIA
oral stimulation of ___: MAMMALINGUS
overdevelopment of ___: MAZAUXESIS
shriveling of ___ from age: MAZORHICNOSIS
small, underdeveloped ___: MASTUNCULI
space between ___: INTERMAZIUM, MEDISECT

DUNG (___)

arousal from contact with ___: COPROLAGNIA
eating ___: COPROPHAGY
writings and drawings involving ___: COPROGRAPHY

HOMOSEXUAL (___)

acceptance of one's ___ orientation: EGO-SYNTONIC HOMOSEXUAL-ITY

anal ___ sex: ANDROSODOMY

anal ___ sex, according to Victorians: GROSS INDECENCY

arousal in heterosexual males from observing female ___ conduct: SAP-PHISMOLAGNY

___ attraction to male adolescents: EPHEBOPHILIA

___ behavior arising from circumstances, including imprisonment: OC-CASIONAL INVERSION

boy used for ___ sex by men: CATAMITE

___ desire by females for the companionship of other women: GY-NECOZYGOUS

estrangement from one's ___ orientation: EGO-DYSTONIC HOMOSEX-UALITY

euphemism for friendship with ___ undertones: PARTICULAR FRIEND-SHIP

face-to-face rubbing between ___ males: FRICTATION

female ___: TRIBADE

female ___ orientation: SAPPHISM

___ interest: HOMOEROTICISM

male ___: CATAPYGON, OSCAR, TAUTANER, URNING

male ___ interested in bulky boys: PHILOBOUPAES

male ___ liking boys in their prime: PHILOMEIRAX

male ___ love: DORIAN LOVE, HELENIC LOVE, ITERANDRIA

___ orientation: EQUISEXUALITY

___ orientation that does not exclude heterosexuality: FACULTATIVE HO-MOSEXUALITY

"___ panic": KEMPF'S DISEASE

seduction of boys by ___ men: PEDOPHTHORIA

to have male ___ intercourse: OSCARIZE

IRRATIONAL FEAR OF (___)

____ being touched: HAPHEPHOBIA
____ breasts being "kneaded" by men: MALAXOPHOBIA
____ childbirth: MAIEUSIOPHOBIA
____ erections: PHALLOPHOBIA
____ erections' being noticed in public: MEDECTOPHOBIA
____ first act of intercourse: ESODOPHOBIA, PRIMESODOPHOBIA
____ hurting female partner while having sex: ANOPHELOPHOBIA
____ lesbians: LESBOPHOBIA
____ men: ANDROPHOBIA
____ naked people: GYMNOPHOBIA
one with ___ kissing: PHILEMAPHOBE
____ penis's being absorbed into one's body: KORO
____ pleasure: HEDONOPHOBIA
____ seeing animals scratch their genitalia or have sex: FAUNADESTIA
____ sex: EROTOPHOBIA, GENOPHOBIA
____ vaginas: KOLPOPHOBIA
____ women: GYNOPHOBIA

KISSING (___)

act of ___: OSCULATION
___ an anus: ANOPHILEMIA
___ armpits: MASCHALOPHILEMIA
___ buttocks: PYGOPHILEMIA
centering one's interest on ___: PHILEMACENTRIC
cold response to ___: PHILEMALGIA
erection from ___: BASORTHOSIS
___ feet: PODOPHILEMIA
hater of ___: MISOPHILEIST
having a mouth sweet enough for ___: HYGROPHILEMATOUS
hunger for ___: PHILEMAMANIA
inducing a desire for ___: PHILEMAGENIC
one fearing or disliking ___: PHILEMAPHOBE
one fond of ___: PHILEMAPHILE
orgasm from ___: BASORGASMUS
pertaining to ___: BASIAL
pertaining to wet ___: HYGROPHILEMATOUS
preferring conventional ___: PHILEMORTHOTIC
___ received with no response: PHERBASIA
___ uncustomary parts of the body: PARAPHILEMIA, PHILEMAXENOSIS
___ with eyes shut: PHILEMYOSIS

MARRIAGE (___)

bad ___: CAGAMOSIS

communal ___ in which all adults are considered married to one another: PANTAGAMY

desire in male for combination of wife and mother in ___: UXOROMATRIA

husband able to have sex only within ___: UXOROSTHEN

husband's being able to have sex only outside his ___: UXORAVALENT

husband's being unable to have sex in ___ because of finding his wife unattractive: UXORONEQUENT

intercourse in ___ between husband and wife: VIRGYNATION

___ of spouses of similar age: ISONOGAMIA

___ outside one's social, ethnic, religious, or cultural group: EXOGAMY

sexual responsiveness in ___: LIBIDOSYNTONIA

spiritual infidelity in ___: PHRENAPISTIA

wife selected for ___ because of physical qualities: GENECLEXIS

___ with asexual living arrangement: AGENOBIOSIS

___ within one's social, ethnic, religious, or cultural group: ENDOGAMY

MASTURBATION (___)

alternative names for ___: SECRET VICE, SELF-ABUSE
___ between two uncircumcised males: DOCKING
___ by crossing and rubbing together female legs: SYNTRIBADISM
___ by female: CLITORIZE, MARITATE
___ by flowing water on vagina: RHEONONIA
___ by rubbing lips of labia majora: AMATRIPSIS
___ by sausages inside vagina: ALLANTOTRIBISM, BOTULINONIA
___ by tickling: ALLELOKNISMUS
excessive ___: CHIROMANIA, MASTURBISM
"mental disorder" from ___: MASTURBOSIS
mentally induced ___: PSYCHIC MASTURBATION
___ of male: MANOTRIPSIS, MANUXORATE
___ of male, especially by female: MULCAGE
___ of male by female hand: CHIRAPSIS

ORAL SEX (___)

alternate names for ___: BUCCAL INTERCOURSE, BUCCAL ONANISM
"deep-throating" ___ on penis: ULTIMATE KISS
female on whom ___ is performed: CUNNILINGANT
female performing ___ on male organ: LÉCHEUSE
female's performing ___ on herself: AUTOCUNNILINGUS
___ in which male inserts penis into another male's mouth: IRRUMATION
___ in which mucous is eaten: MUCOPHAGY
male performing ___ on penis: FELLATOR
male performing ___ on vagina: LÉCHEUR
male's performing ___ on his own penis: AUTOFELLATIO
___ on anus: HEDRALINGUS
___ on armpits: MASCHALINGUS
___ on eyeball: OCULOLINCTUS
___ on nipples: THELELINGUS
___ on nose: NASOLINGUS
___ on penis: FELLATIO, PENILINGUS, PHALLOSUGIA, VIRILINGUS
___ on vagina: CUNNILINGUS, OROLABIAL STIMULATION
performer of ___ on vagina: CUNNILINGUIST

ORGASM(S) (___)

ability in males to delay ___: LAGNODOMNIA
___ difficult for males: DYSORGASMIA
dissatisfaction after ___: LAGNECHIA
faster ___ than usual: TACHORGASMIA
female ___: GYNACME
___ from watching others make love: ALLOPELLIA
inducing or promoting ___: ORGASMOGENIC
induction of an ___: ACMEGENESIS
___ occurring in sleep as a "wet dream:" ONEIROGMUS
___ only after much effort: TARDORGASMUS
painful ___ in males: ALGORGASMIA
seminal discharge without ___: ACONORRHEA
simultaneous ___ in a couple: SYNORGASMIA
___ without ejaculation: KENORGASMY

PENIS(ES) (___)

condition of a downward-curving ___: CHORDEE
condition of having a circumcised ___: ACUCULLOPHALLIA
condition of having a large ___: MACROPHALLIA
condition of having a soft and non-erectible ___: HAPALOPHALLIA
condition of having an erect ___ at night: NOCTORTHOSIS
condition of having an erect ___ bulging in one's pants: MEDECTASIA
cosmetologist for ___: MEDOCURIX
fear of losing the hardness of one's erect ___: MEDOMALACOPHOBIA
fear that others will notice one's erect ___ through one's pants: MEDEC-
TOPHOBIA
fondness for circumcised ___: ACUCULLOPHILIA
gentle lovemaking by ___: MEDOCHNOIA
having a long ___: DOLICHOPHALLIC
having a pointed ___: ACULEOPHALLIC
having a spiny ___: ACANTHOPHALLIC
impotence of ___ from man's worry: KEDAVALENCE
large ___: MACROPHALLUS
licking the ___: PHALLINGUS, VIRILINGUS
long-lasting erection of ___: PERDUROTHOSIS
obscene language about ___: MEDOLALIA, PHALLOLALIA
obsession with the ___: MENTULOMANIA, MENTULOPHRENIA
overfrequent use of ___ for sex: PHALLACRASIA
pain in ___ from pushing in an overnarrow vagina: DIAPIRESALGIA
painful erection of ___: ITHYALGIA
pertaining to a depiction of an erect ___ on a statue: ITHYPHALLIC
pertaining to, or having, an erect ___: APELLOUS, ORTHOPHALLIC
pride or pleasure in possessing a ___: MENTULHEDONIA
pulling on one's ___ habitually: PEOTILLOMANIA
small ___: HOMUNK
soft condition of ___ after loss of erection: DETUMESCENCE
uncircumcised ___: GOY TOY
underdeveloped ___: HYPOMEDIA
woman who thinks obsessively about ___: MENTULOPHRENIAC

PROSTITUTE(S) (___)

government by ___: PORNOCRACY
Latin name for ___: LUPAE
Latin name for house of ___: LUPANAR
love of ___: PORNEPHILIA
lover of ___: PHILOPORNIST
old Latin term for ___: MERETRIX
old name for ___: QUEAN

SEXUAL INTERCOURSE (___)

able to perform ___ face down only: PRONOVALENT
able to perform ___ face up only: SUPINOVALENT
able to perform ___ in morning only: MANEVALENT
able to perform ___ only with wife: UXOROVALENT
able to perform ___ only with women other than one's wife: UXORAVA-
LENT
able to perform ___ while lying down only: CLINOVALENT
able to perform ___ while standing only: STASIVALENT
active partner in anal ___: INDORSER
___ among three persons: TROILISM
anal ___: ARSOMETRY, BUGGERY, GROSS INDECENCY, NINETY-NINE
anal ___ performed on oneself: AUTOPEDERASTY
anal ___ with female: ANOMEATIA
another name for ___: INTROMISSION, PHALLATION
___ attended by pain in genitalia, especially in males: DYSPHALLATION
belief in reserving ___ for procreation only: ATERPSIA
believer in brief ___: HAPLOIST
___ between father and daughter: THYGATRIA
___ between human being and animal: BESTIALITY
___ between husband and unwilling wife: VAGINORAPTUS
___ between husband and wife: VIRGYNATION
___ between two females rubbing genitals together: TRIBADISM
boy who is used for anal ___ with a man: CATAMITE
brief ___: BRACHYCUBIA
centering one's interest on ___: COITOCENTRIC
centering one's interest on the foreplay of ___: PAIZOCENTRIC
compulsive desire for ___: HYPERPHILIA
condomless ___: GYMNOPHALLATION, OMOCOINIA
conventional ___: ORTHOCUBIA
demon assuming the shape of female and having ___ with a sleeping
male: SUCCUBUS
demon assuming the shape of male and having ___ with a sleeping
woman: INCUBUS
depression in some women from first act of ___ and consequent loss of
virginity: HYMENOPENTHY
expert on technique of ___: DEONTEUR
fear of ___: COITOPHOBIA
female participant in ___: COITANTE

first act of ___: PRIMESODIA

___ for pleasure only: ***COITUS DELICATUS***

hunger for ___: COITOLIMIA

___ in a car: AMOMAXIA

___ in a filled bathtub: COITOBALNISM

___ in an orgy: ***COITUS BACCHICUS***

___ in which female matches the upward and downward movements of male: ISODROMIA

___ in which female thrusts her genitalia upward as the male thrusts his downward: HETERODROMIA

___ in which female welcomes male: ***COITUS ACCEPTUS***

___ in which male withdraws penis from vagina before ejaculation: ***COITUS INTERRUPTUS***

___ in which male withholds ejaculation: ***COITUS RESERVATUS***

___ in wooded area: DASOFALLATION

knowledge of expert phallic techniques of ___: DECOROMEDIA

loss of desire to complete ___ because of partner's bad breath: HALITALAGNIA

male able to perform ___ only once within a given period: UNIVALEUR

male boast about having ___ with a particular female: JACTITATION

male engaging in anal ___ with a female: ANORAST

male inability to perform ___ due to worry: KEDAVALENCE

male preferring to perform ___ while standing: STASOPHALLIST

male preferring to perform ___ with a fully clothed woman: ENDYTOPHALLIST

"mental disorder" in male from not having enough ___ with women: AMULIEROSIS

missionary position of ___ with female's legs wrapped around male's loins: OCEANIC POSITION

mistress who has ___ with a priest: PARNEL

newlywed virgin's pain from first act of ___: NEOGAMALGIA

orgiastic ___: ***COITUS BACCHICUS***

"orthodox" or conventional ___: ORTHOCUBIA

"overfrequent" ___: ACROCOITION, COITOPERISSIA

penis's sensation of being snatched or snapped by the vagina during ___: KYSTAPAZA

pertaining to "promiscuous" or illicit ___: PAPHIAN

preferring ___ while reclining: RECUMBOFAVIA

___ producing pregnancy: ***COITUS FECUNDUS***

relating to occupying the top position in ___: INCUBOUS

sensation of having the penis tightly embraced during ___: KOLPOCIN-
GULAPHORIA
slow ___: BRADYCUBIA
sore caused by friction on genitals during ___: COITAL ECTRIMMA
to perform ___ with a spacious vagina: VOLUTATE
"uncontrollable" desire in women for ___: NYMPHOMANIA
vaginal pain during ___ stemming from stretching to accommodate the
penis: KOLPEURYNTALGIA
woman who has ___ for money: QUEAN

VAGINA(S) (___)

ability of ___ to be penetrated: INGRESSABILITY
another name for a ___: INTROITUS, QUIM
dilation of ___: COLPECTASIA
dryness of ___: COLPOXEROSIS
enlarged condition of clitoris of ___: CLITOROMEGALY
erection of clitoris of ___: SEXUAL EBURNATION
fear of ___: KOLPOPHOBIA
having a beautiful ___: CALLICUNNATE
having a hairless ___: ACOMOVULVATE
kiss ___: CUNNIPHILEMIA
licker of ___: CUNNILINGUIST
lubricating secretion of ___: HUMEX
obscene conversations about ___: CUNNILALIA
pain from stretching ___ to accommodate penis: KOLPEURYNTALGIA
pain in ___: COLPALGIA
pain in ___ during contraction: VAGINISMUS
penis's entrapment in ___: *PENIS CAPTIVUS*
pertaining to clitoris of ___: BALANIC
preferring hairless ___: ACOMOCLITIC
rubbing of ___ by a man: CUNNITRIPSIS
scratching, rubbing of ___: CUNNORASIA
self-moistening of ___: MADEFACTION
sensation given by ___ of snapping the male organ: KYSTAPAZA
spastic contraction of ___: COLPISMUS
stretching, dilation of ___: KOLPECTASIA
sweet smellingness of ___: DULCICUNNIA
tickling a ___: CUNNIKNISMOS
to finger ___: DACTYLATE
to think excessively about ___: COLPOPHRONATE
well-moistened condition of ___: CHYMOCUNNIA
wig of ___: MERKIN
___ with condition of thick hymen: PACHYHYMENIA

VIRGIN(S) (___)

another name for a ___: PARTHENA
defiler of ___: STUPRATOR
depression by former ___ from losing virginity: HYMENOPENTHY
fear of ___: PARTHENOPHOBIA
female not a ___: PHALLATA
female technically a ___ but with much sexual experience: DEMI-VIERGE, PENULTIMA
having a vagina of a ___: PARTHENOCOLPIA
intercourse with a ___: PARTHENOCLASIS
male attracted only to ___: PARTHENOPHILE
seducer of ___: PARTHENOCLEPT

BIBLIOGRAPHY

The American Heritage Dictionary of the English Language. Boston: Houghton Mifflin Co., 1992.

Beeching, Cyril. *A Dictionary of Eponyms.* 2d ed. New York: Oxford University Press, 1988.

Berent, Irwin M., and Rod L. Evans. *More Weird Words.* New York: Berkley Books, 1995.

Berent, Irwin M., and Rod L. Evans. *Weird Words.* New York: Berkley Books, 1995.

Black, Henry Campbell. *Black's Law Dictionary.* St. Paul, MN: West Publishing Co., 1979.

Bowler, Peter. *The Superior Person's Book of Words.* New York: Dell Laurel, 1982.

Brown, Roland Wilbur. *Composition of Scientific Words.* Washington, DC: Smithsonian Institution Press, 1956.

Bullough, Vern, and Bonnie Bullough. *Sin, Sickness, and Sanity: A History of Sexual Attitudes.* New York: New American Library, 1977.

Byrne, Josepha Heifitz. *Mrs. Byrne's Dictionary of Unusual, Obscure, and Preposterous Words.* New York: Citadel Press, 1974.

Dickson, Paul. *Words.* New York: Delacorte Press, 1982.

Dorland's Illustrated Medical Dictionary, 26th ed. Philadelphia: W. B. Saunders Co., 1981.

Ellis, Havelock. *Studies in the Psychology of Sex.* New York: Random House, 1936.

Evans, Rod L., and Irwin M. Berent. *Getting Your Words' Worth.* New York: Warner Books, 1993.

Francoeur, Robert T., Martha Cornog, Timothy Perper, and Norman Scherzer, eds. *The Complete Dictionary of Sexology.* New York: Continuum, 1995.

Gause, John T. *The Complete University Word Hunter.* New York: Thomas Y. Crowell Co., 1967.

Goldenson, Robert M., and Kenneth N. Anderson. *Sex A to Z.* New York: World Almanac, 1989.

Grambs, David. *The Endangered English Dictionary.* New York: W. W. Norton & Co., 1994.

Green, Jonathon. *The Big Book of Filth.* London: Cassell, 1999.

Handford, S. A., and Mary Herberg. *Langenscheidt's Pocket Latin Dictionary*. Berlin, 1966.

Hellweg, Paul. *The Insomniac's Dictionary*. New York: Ballantine Books, 1986.

Hill, Robert H., ed. *A Dictionary of Difficult Words*. Rev. ed. New York: Gramercy Publishing Co., 1990.

Lewis, Norman. *The Comprehensive Word Guide*. Garden City, NY: Doubleday, 1958.

Love, Brenda. *Encyclopedia of Unusual Sex Practices*. New York: Barricade Books, 1992.

Money, John. *Lovemaps*. Irvington, NY: Prometheus Books, 1986.

Novabatzky, Peter, and Ammon Shea. *Depraved English*. New York: St. Martin's Press, 1999.

Partridge, Eric. *Origins: A Short Etymological Dictionary of Modern English*. New York: Greenwich House, 1983.

Pei, Mario, Salvatore Ramondino, and Laura Torbet. *Dictionary of Foreign Terms*. New York: Dell, 1974.

Rocke, Russell. *The Grandiloquent Dictionary*. Englewood Cliffs, NJ: Prentice-Hall, 1972.

Schachner, Robert, and John Whited. *Lost Words of the English Language*. Holbrook, MA: Bob Adams, 1989.

Schmidt, J. E. *The Lecher's Lexicon*. New York: Bell Publishing Co., 1967.

Schur, Norman W. *1000 Most Obscure Words*. New York: Facts on File, 1990.

Smith, Robert W. L. *Dictionary of English Word-Roots*. Totowa, NJ: Littlefield, Adams & Co., 1966.

Urdang, Lawrence, ed. *Everyday Reader's Dictionary of Misunderstood, Misused, Mispronounced Words*. New York: Quadrangle/The New York Times Book Co., 1972.

Urdang, Lawrence. *Modifiers*. Detroit: Gale Research Co., 1982.

Webster's Third New International Dictionary. Springfield, MA: G. & C. Merriam Co., 1971.